RAISE YOUR VOICE

DK

DK

RAISE YOUR VOICE

MAKE YOURSELF HEARD IN A NOISY WORLD

CURATED BY NADIA JAE

FEATURING:
AMY DOWDEN • KIA PEGG
GREG JAMES • JJ CHALMERS
ROMAN KEMP • GEORGE THE POET
ADE ADEPITAN • MOLLIE KING
DANNY WALTERS • EDITH BOWMAN
NANCY KACUNGIRA • RUTH MADELEY
ZARA MCDERMOTT • AMAR LATIF

I dedicate this book to the younger
me – thank you; so proud of us.
We stayed true to ourself and our voice.
Now, we get to use it doing something
we love every day.

Thank you to my parents, family,
and friends for allowing me to be
myself and loving me regardless.

To Ky, my messenger, my angel. May
the ceiling of my success be the floor of
yours. You changed my life. Thank you
for choosing me to be your mum.

Nadia Jae

CONTENTS

WAIT!

We're so glad you're here, and we wanted to share some important information with you before you read on.

Each of the interviews in this book explores personal experiences about real things that happened to real people. Some of them cover topics that could make you feel anxious or upset. These experiences might remind you of things you've been through, or things that people you care about have been through.

It's okay to put the book down, clear your head, and come back whenever you feel ready to read some more.

If you need support around any of the issues described in this book, you can find out about some great organizations and get more information by visiting: www.bbc.co.uk/actionline.

NADIA JAE

Here is how I found my voice....

Who is Nadia Jae?

It's funny, I spent the first years of my life being told to be quiet. "Nadia, you aren't in the playground any more. Stop talking!" My teacher would yell that at me when I chatted continuously during class. Another primary school teacher of mine used to call me a "busybody", and to be honest, she was right. I absolutely loved talking, whether it was about celebrities, trivia, or how I planned to take over the world. Little Nadia Jae was never shy when it came to speaking.

My mum would often joke about how talkative I was at family gatherings. She would refer to what she called her "cherished moments of calm" before she used to pick me up from school. The story goes that as soon as I got in the car, mum would tell me to wait until we got home before she allowed me to talk. We had these armchairs in the living room and I would perch right underneath my mum's armpit, wait for her to say "Okay Nad, how was your day?" and I'd launch into my latest day-in-the-life episode.

Her favourite stories were about the new boy in my class called "Necklace". The boy's name was Nicholas but I was having none of it aged five. That and the time I complained about not having chocolate milk upon arrival at school any more (showing political awareness at the recent change of government), and asking her why she wouldn't let me go to school by myself (my reasoning being that there weren't any monsters on the road to school, so I should be fine). My aunty would often chime in with additional memories of me reading books to my cousins and changing my voice to suit each character. This behaviour displayed at a young age has stuck with me right into my thirties. Not only did I feel confident in who I was, but the adults around me knew who I was too. I was a young, bright, talkative child who was headstrong, naive, and very observant.

My teachers, parents, and other well-meaning adults encouraged me to be myself while giving me a lifelong lesson: there is a time and a place for everything, even when it comes to talking. That place may not be at the cinema, the classroom, the library, or at home badgering my mum after a hard day's work, but on the radio? Could this be where I would be in my element with nobody censoring me? A place where I could genuinely be myself and be congratulated for it? If only I knew I would make a living from being myself all those years ago.

As well as being a chatterbox, I seemed to have energy sourced from batteries, so I was always on the go. My parents sent me to stage school and I quickly learned that acting wasn't my strength because of my uncontrollable urge to come out of character. I tried singing and I could hold a note or two, but it wasn't where I found joy. I was enrolled in dance classes from age five and had fallen into dance because it came so naturally to me. I always thought I would be a professional dancer, career-wise. Now I realize I was learning to navigate myself in society just by knowing what I liked and disliked – including music, clothes, boys, subjects, and even food – all of which was part of me finding my voice and my place.

I was really lucky. I was always encouraged by those around me to pursue my artistic passions. I had quite a liberal upbringing; my stepdad would spend hours running around dropping me to

"There is a time and a place for everything, even when it comes to talking. That place may not be at the cinema, in the classroom, at the library, or at home badgering my mum after a hard day's work, but on the radio?"

classes, auditions etc, whilst my mum enjoyed watching all the performances and showing me off to the aunties, uncles, and anyone who would listen. Having parental support really helped my confidence. I was a naturally outgoing and bubbly child, and those characteristics aren't always nurtured by adults, whether because of a lack of knowledge, time, or even interest. The confidence to speak out and be yourself can grow from feeling safe in your environment, feeling able to report wrongdoings to adults, and having friends who feel as brave and empowered as you do. It can even come from admiring strong protagonists in TV shows and films. Luckily, I already had this confidence inside me and, encouraged by my family from an early age, it has enabled me to make choices that serve me positively today.

Learning when to use my voice

I never had any issues speaking up, but my first memory of seeing what it looks like in others was my best friend at primary school, Annabel. She ran towards me one day in a rage and told me she had experienced something that I was completely uneducated about: racism. This was my first encounter with the term and I remember it vividly. A few of us huddled around Annabel while she proceeded to explain, using the vocabulary of a seven-year-old, that someone had "cussed her colour". Ignorance really is bliss, because I was really confused. I listened to my friend and wondered what could possibly be so bad about a colour, not realising that my friend was verbalising being racially abused, and the colour she spoke of was our race.

"Somehow, I found the strength and I stood up for myself. I hadn't discouraged her bullying shenanigans before, but I knew I was definitely not going to be a victim of them."

I genuinely watched in confusion as we approached the teacher to explain what had happened. Annabel cried while relaying the story, but I saw her stand up for herself and call out something she knew was wrong, which naturally had an effect on me. Even as a small child, I was being exposed to things that would empower me to speak up when I needed to. I admit, this didn't always happen, but the importance of defending yourself was definitely ingrained in me that day.

Once I entered the real lion's den, an all-girls secondary school, I was faced with a real test of character. I hate to adhere to stereotypes, but all us girls did was talk. We'd talk about each other, to each other, and then be confrontational about who talked to who first about one another. Then we'd ask each other why we spoke to someone else instead of to one another! Phew! It was tiring! I managed to stay afloat for the majority of Year 7 and 8 until my day finally came. I remember being targeted by the school bully, who I now realize with hindsight was quite hard done by in life. She had little money, no home boundaries, struggled with grades at school, and put on a bravado so that no one could bully her first. Regardless, at age 14 none of this mattered to me or her because today it was my turn to be on the receiving end of her verbal abuse.

We were in the Year Room on our lunch break and I was fed up with her having regular digs at my friends. She would come over, grab our food, laugh at our clothes, hair, or anything that would belittle us. Usually, I would ignore her because it wasn't directed at me, but we had all had enough. I told a friend what I thought of her and it got back to said bully, so naturally she confronted me about it in front of the entire lunch room. Somehow, I found the strength and I stood up for myself. I hadn't discouraged her bullying shenanigans before, but I knew I was definitely not going to be a victim of them. I needed her and everyone watching to know that too.

I have no idea what ancestor was watching over me that day, but the response I got was not what I expected. She cursed me back a bit and then she left me alone. From then on when I saw her, we exchanged a smirk or a weird smile and eventually, after a few years we became loose friends. I set boundaries and she had accepted them. One nil to me and my voice!

Trusting my inner voice

I always refer to my inner voice as my intuition or my "gut feeling". Your intuition literally means "a feeling that you are being taught from within" and it is something you grow to trust. When you feel in your stomach that something great is going to occur, trust that feeling. In time, you'll also learn to trust that sinking feeling in your gut when you know something really isn't right for you.

"In time, you'll also learn to trust that sinking feeling in your gut when you know something really isn't right for you."

I have had a few positive experiences that came from listening to my gut. The biggest example by far has to be deciding to become a mother. For context, I was in my second year of university in Luton after deciding to leave the course I was doing in London because it wasn't fulfilling (another example of when I listened to my gut). This turned out to be a life-changing decision, as I met my son's father. He was Annabel's (yes, that same best friend!) neighbour whilst we lived on campus.

I was in the middle of my studies and dating my son's father when I suspected I was pregnant. I went to the nurse on campus and was given two free pregnancy tests. They were both negative, so I continued to live my best student life. It wasn't until one day I put on a pair of slim-fitting jeans and realized they were a struggle to button up that I suspected something. When I looked down, I saw my typically inward belly button now protruding forward and looking up at me like an eyeball. I was 19 and I remember thinking, "Do belly buttons change when you turn 20?" Because there was no other explanation at that point.

Annabel and I bought a really expensive third-time-lucky test just to be sure. Lo and behold, the test was positive. Again, my overactive imagination wondered if someone could be pulling a prank, because there was no way I was really having a baby. But not only was I pregnant, I was already 13 weeks gone and didn't have a lot of time to make a decision. My son's dad was pretty supportive at first but didn't help much after that, and I quickly realized I had to decide what to do on my own.

I booked to have a termination as I felt that it was bad timing to have a child. I was 19, at university, living away from my family, and without any savings, so of course this was the right thing to do. But as I sat in the waiting room, my gut was the loudest I had ever heard it. This didn't feel right for me. I left without going through with my consultation, but I still wasn't sure what to do, so I left it for a few days.

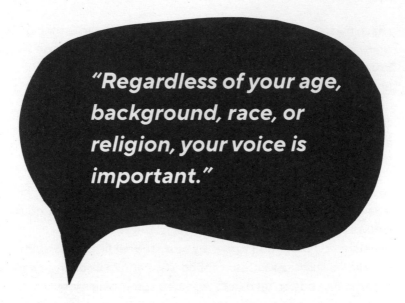

"Regardless of your age, background, race, or religion, your voice is important."

I then decided to do something I have never done before – pray. I asked God out loud if he was real, and could hear me, then could he give me a sign as to what I should do. This was actually a time when I didn't immediately trust my gut as deep down I knew what I wanted to do, but fear had taken over.

A few more days passed after my loud-and-out prayer and I was making my way to uni when a white van stopped in front of me. I remember being agitated as it was blocking my way and I was already late for class. The van had a sticker on the back of it that said "PEEK". I thought it was quite random but I went about my day. Later in class, I thought about that van and its sticker. Why that word: "PEEK"? No branding, no explanation, no other stickers. Curious, I jotted it down on my notepad and suddenly realized that if I reversed the word is spelt "KEEP". I was stunned. I jolted up, excused myself from class, and called my friend. I couldn't believe it. It was the sign I'd asked for.

Needless to say, keeping my baby was literally the best decision of my life. My friends and family were extremely supportive and my son was born that August. I went back to university, got my degree, and he was in attendance at my graduation ceremony. From that day, I vowed to always listen to my gut.

The work needed to feel confident in yourself and your beliefs will continue as your character and personality develop. You will find yourself in situations that require you to speak up in order to stand up for yourself and feel seen. Whether you are dealing with family, teachers and classmates at school, or colleagues in the workplace, once you know the fundamentals about yourself you will find it easier to navigate the world. I really believe I knew who I was at age 5, but it took me till I was 25 to know how to navigate that properly in society. Some people don't know until they are 45! But regardless of your age, background, race, or religion, nobody is you or can speak for you. And, as you learn and grow, remember, there is nothing wrong with changing your mind. Your voice at one stage in life may differ from the one at another time in your life.

One thing I learned as I got older is that talking about something wasn't the only thing I could do. If you feel strongly about something, shouting or tweeting about it isn't the only way to be heard. Sometimes, starting an anonymous petition, donating to a cause, rallying others into action, or even simply writing a direct email, can be just as powerful.

But, regardless of your age, background, race, or religion, your voice is important. We have so many influences around us: friends, social media, people we look up to, siblings, teachers, and parents. Sometimes it's difficult to admit to them and the world that our views are different. It can be hard speaking up for what feels right for you if it puts you in challenging situations or people dislike you because of it. Your views contribute to a myriad of voices that often make conversations and situations more exciting!

Fighting fear

I now get to use my voice every day doing a job I love. Not everybody is lucky enough to be able to do that, and whilst I am super blessed, I also sacrificed and worked hard to get here. I currently host the *BBC 1Xtra Breakfast Show*, a job that really is a dream come true. I get to wake the nation up, play music, spread light and love, interact with people, and finish work at 10am. Sweet! What people don't see though, is that my job entails lots of work off air, such as prep time with my producers, and waking up at 5am every morning! (If you're lucky my outfit matches, and on a really good day, my hair is done.) And getting the job of my dreams wasn't easy.

I found a great part-time job in Tech PR, which worked around me raising my son. The problem was, because the job was highly paid, I wasn't eligible to receive government support – but the job's wage also didn't cover enough for us to live comfortably. So I moved out of my two-bedroom flat, and back with my parents. This was one of the best things to happen because I bought myself a DJ Controller to cheer myself up and learned how to DJ, and my career began to take off.

I joined 1Xtra in October 2018 as part of the residency line-up. Myself and four other presenters shared a Wednesday-night slot, which meant I was on air for two hours a month. Before this, I had worked for the community radio Westside FM which I left in 2014 to join Bang Radio (aka The Beat London), where I spent five years. It wasn't easy, I had my son at afterschool club so I could do the daytime slot, and it was unpaid with no guarantee of making it to a professional level. So when I was offered the 1Xtra Residency it literally changed my life. My first paid show at 1Xtra for two hours work was equivalent to a whole month of pay from my weekday shows at The Beat, where only my expenses were covered. It was a dream come true.

Another dream was fulfilled when I was asked to do my first cover show for the legend Trevor Nelson. I was absolutely bricking it! This was not just a legend's show but also my first live show on 1Xtra. It went amazingly well and I was complimented heavily for it by my colleagues. I went on to cover daytime Sunday shows regularly, which resulted in me gaining my own show *Weekend Breakfast* in October 2019, just a year after joining the station.

So, fast forward to the hardest year of our lives. In July 2020, the current *Breakfast Show* presenter, Dotty, announced she was leaving, so I was asked to cover the show for a month while they looked for a presenter. However, a month of covering turned into two months. Two months turned into three. I became attached to the show, the listeners, and used to the early weekday mornings. I didn't want to go back to Weekend Breakfast anymore and I felt like I was good enough to present the show on my own. For the first time in my life, I was forced to use my voice to fight for the career I wanted. And surprisingly, speaking up for myself wasn't the first reaction. Something that usually came so naturally to me was now a cognitive process. Why couldn't I just SAY I wanted the show? My career at 1Xtra felt so fast-tracked, was I really ready to take on the biggest show on the network?

The truth is, I'd convinced myself that I didn't deserve it when deep down I knew it was something I could do. And for some reason, that strong voice I had displayed in my childhood was suddenly very quiet. Everybody else's voice was so loud in support of me, why was I now afraid to dream big?

It happens. Doubt can always creep in. It was a strange time, at the start of the Covid pandemic, so I gave myself grace. The loud and confident me knew the stakes were high and I guess I was scared. And that's okay. Once I spoke to my family, friends (I did this constantly – they all deserve medals), and production team (who all reassured me of my ability), I found my voice again and let people know, I wanted the show. Now, I use that voice every morning to wake up the nation.

I've had lots of moments of uncertainty in my life, but getting my dream job was the moment I teetered the most. I attended three universities and had my son bang smack in the middle of my degree. I left a full-time retail job to pursue a career in the arts with no savings or an actual plan. I had countless part-time jobs to fund my unpaid radio hobby, whilst having a 6-year-old and trying to run a household without a partner. Piece of cake!
(I hope you can sense the sarcasm here.)

> *"I went from being told off for my constant need to talk to those traits being the exact tools I need for my dream job."*

Everything I have experienced, from childhood into adulthood, has helped me to feel confident in who I am and what I want to say. I went from being told off for my constant need to talk to those traits being the exact tools I need for my dream job.

I cannot begin to tell you how amazing it feels when trusting and listening to yourself pays off. The majority of people overcame their own personal struggles to get to where they are now and it has paid off in more ways than one.

There are many stories and experiences in this book that I hope you can draw inspiration and learn from. And if your circumstances right now don't permit you to do what you'd love to do, it doesn't mean it won't happen for you. If you want to be a doctor, lawyer, pilot, vet, music producer, app developer, scientist, blogger, photographer, window cleaner, driver... whatever inspires you and feels good to you... I want you to know that your inner voice will never lie to you. Find it. Follow it. Nurture it. Listen to it.

Now, go and be great.

KNOW YOURSELF

1

KNOW YOURSELF

Essentially, to know yourself is to manoeuvre through life the best way you know how. I always refer to "my inner voice" when it comes to knowing myself. Have you been in a tricky situation and you can almost hear a voice speaking to you inside your head? That is YOU. It is the core of you telling you what feels good and what doesn't; what is right or wrong and what you can and can't do. It's different in everyone and it's also what makes us all so unique. Feeling confident about who we are is one of the hardest things to do because we are constantly changing. The process may be tough, but it can also be an exciting, wonderful journey of self-discovery; one which I personally have enjoyed from a young age.

RUTH MADELEY

Ruth Madeley is a BAFTA nominated actress, named as one of BAFTA's Breakthrough Brits in 2017. Ruth gained notoriety in 2019 for her performance as "Rosie" in the critically acclaimed BBC One/HBO series *Years and Years*. In 2018, Ruth presented a BBC Two/Horizon documentary *Spina Bifida & Me* which examined how a law could prevent many birth defects and how pioneering foetal surgery could transform the lives of babies with spina bifida.

Q **So how did you become an actress? When did it start for you?**

A Well, my road into this industry wasn't traditional in any way, shape or form. Before I started acting professionally, my acting credentials had started and finished with being Mary in my primary school nativity play. I didn't go to drama school and never had a single acting class. I was a writer. I loved storytelling and was creative so I studied that at university. My vision was always that I'd be a script writer, but I guess the universe had other ideas.

I was doing some work experience at the BBC, and a producer asked me to go to an audition for a wheelchair user in a CBBC drama. It was just for one episode and they thought it would be easy because I was there – I think any wheelchair user would have done. I went along purely to be nosy, never thinking that I would get the role. I wanted to learn more about the industry and this was a good way to meet the producer, the director, and the writer and learn a bit about how they cast things. But I ended up getting the role. I'd always thought actors were insane – why on earth would they put themselves through the torture of the audition process? But as soon as I got in the room, I had that adrenaline rush, and I understood it. And as soon as I stepped on set, I really loved it. Learning about all the different roles and seeing how a drama was made really interested me. Though I still didn't think of it as a career; it was just something to do on the side and a way to make contacts and some extra money. I got another little role on Jack Whitehall's *Fresh Meat*, but that was it. There was nothing. And then, a few years ago, a script by Jack Thorn called *Don't Take My Baby* landed on my agent's desk. The lead role was for a wheelchair user and casting were seeing loads of different people. You didn't have to have masses of experience – they wanted to see as many people as possible because disabled actors still are underrepresented. I remember my agent saying that if I got this, everything would change. And that was six or seven years ago.

Q Tell me about growing up with a disability and how that shaped your view of the world. Did you ever doubt that you would be able to do what you wanted to?

A I grew up being the only disabled person in my primary school so I always knew I was different. Of course, there are times when you get really frustrated and really bothered by it, but on the whole I never saw myself as being anything other than successful. I'm unashamedly stubborn and determined. I think that, as a disabled kid, you have this built-in resilience because you're living in a world that's constantly telling you that you can't do things or you're not going to be able to achieve the same level as your non-disabled peers. And I just refused to believe or accept that narrative.

"You learn to live in such a creative way, finding different ways to do things."

I grew up with a mum, dad, and sister who were very, very supportive and never treated me any differently because of my disability. They never said, "You can't do it." They would say, "Right, we'll find a different way to do it." That was just the way my childhood was, and I carried that with me into

adult life. Things might take me a bit longer and I'll have to be creative in how I do it, but I'll do it. And I'll do it well.

You learn to live in such a creative way, finding different ways to do things. Hopefully that's helped my creativity now in my career. Disabled kids often have ingenious ways of finding their way through everything because this world is not built for disabled people. You're constantly coming up against inaccessibility, and it's a skill to be able to find new ways to do things.

Q **Which you've mastered. I mean, you're currently BAFTA nominated, which is absolutely huge and maybe it leads into my next question. Can you tell me about a big achievement of yours?**

A So probably the BAFTA nomination was the biggest achievement that I can think of – it's so prestigious and unexpected. Disabled talent is very rarely given roles or the platform to be at that level in the industry. So to even be nominated was unbelievably overwhelming, as was being on stage and seeing all these people who I've watched on TV for years, all looking at me. I remember saying to my family that these people have no idea who I am, but after this they will, which blew my mind. So that was a big achievement, prestige-wise.

But one of my biggest achievements is a bit more basic in that it's being able to do this as a job – to pay my mortgage this way. I've had so many different jobs, and now to be able to say that I make my living by acting is a really big deal for me – from a personal and also a creative perspective.

> *"I think self-care is so important, especially in today's world."*

Q It's an amazing feeling. And what about something that's challenged you? How did you overcome it?

A Disabled people live with lots of different health conditions, but for me personally, my disability is spina bifida and scoliosis, which means that I have a lot of pain. Managing that in the best way possible, and alongside my work, is really hard. As positive as you are, there are days when the pain is just rubbish, absolutely rubbish, and there's nothing you can do other than sit there and just write it off as a bad day. But that's mentally very hard to deal with, especially when the pain messes with your sleep. How have I overcome that? Each time it happens, you just do because there is no other choice. I wish I had some pearls of wisdom for people. Anybody dealing with health problems like that has to factor it into everyday life and work. And again, as a disabled person, it's something that I just deal with. I often try to do something really nice for myself. If I have to lie down for a couple of days because my pain is that bad, then there's always online shopping. I can buy myself a treat to cheer myself up. I can cuddle with my dog. I can ask my boyfriend to make me some really nice food. Just something that feels good. I think self-care is so important, especially in today's world. When you're on set, sometimes there is that element of ploughing through, but it's about what you do after the job's finished. I have to make sure I factor that in. I used to push myself through, but now, in my 30s, I'm learning to listen to my body. I have to if I want to be able to keep doing this as a career. As a kid, I wouldn't stop and I'd refuse to ask for help. I definitely wish I'd know more about self-care when I was younger, but it's never too late.

"I soon realized that I had to use my voice. I had to speak up about authentic representation and about what's needed on set so that the next disabled person who came into a job after me wouldn't have to deal with some of the same rubbish."

Q That's a great answer. Thank you, Ruth. I wonder if there was ever a time where you've used your voice to speak up for something or someone?

A As you know, disabled people are severely underrepresented in this industry. I've been very blessed to have had the success I've had in such a short time. At the start, I was very reluctant to be a spokesperson on disability in the industry because I didn't feel I was qualified. I know pretty much everything there is to know about my own disability, but not anyone else's. There are so many different disabilities. And even if a person has the same one as you, it doesn't affect them in the same way. But I soon realized that I had to use my voice. I had to speak up about authentic representation and about what's needed on set so that the next disabled person who came into a job after me wouldn't have to deal with some of the same rubbish. You don't always want to be the teacher – you just want to do your job. But at the same time, there's a certain amount of education you have to give people. I learned from other people about things on set, so if someone can learn from me about how to be more inclusive and make the environment more accessible on their next job, then that's when I can lend my voice for positive change.

But it doesn't just have to be in the industry – it's also about challenging people's perceptions about disability in general. I was in a taxi once and the driver asked me about my disability and whether it was hereditary. I answered that it wasn't – it had just popped up. He said, "Oh, you're so unlucky. I'm so sorry," but I replied that I'm lucky because I get a blue badge, which means free parking everywhere. So it's really fun to challenge people's perceptions about

KNOW YOURSELF

disabilities – there are lots of positives that come with it. And it's fun to use your voice to make people smile and think, "Oh, she's not depressed. She's not living a rubbish life. She's living a good one, and the disability is part of that."

Q **Yeah, there are lots of able-bodied people who are miserable. And it's got nothing to do with the ability to do stuff.**

A I mean, the time when I'm most miserable is when I've not had my morning coffee. And that has zero to do with my disability!

Q **And what would you say to young Ruth now? Do you have any words of wisdom?**

A I would say that you're going to have some really rubbish times with your health, but the stuff on the other side of that is going to be more than you could ever have imagined. So just keep going. Don't be so damn hard on yourself. You're doing your best, you're learning, and you've got so much that you can and will achieve. Don't be scared of it. Lean in and just go with it. Don't be scared of it.

"I learned that it was really important to have that conversation and say, "Actually, I'm struggling a bit here."

GREG JAMES

"The journey for me was a process of remembering those parts of who I was, rather than becoming something else... a series of events that encouraged me to become more of myself, of who I really am."

NANCY KACUNGIRA

"And this is one thing I learned: you can't get anywhere on your own. You need your community, your tribe."

ADE ADEPITAN

"I definitely wish I'd known more about self-care when I was younger, but it's never too late."

RUTH MADELEY

NANCY KACUNGIRA

Nancy Kacungira has worked in radio and television in Kenya, Uganda, and Tanzania. She currently reports for *BBC World News* from across Africa and beyond. Nancy won the BBC World News Komla Dumor Award in 2015, and the Women For Africa International Award in 2016 for her work challenging stereotypes and misconceptions. She holds a Master's degree in International Communications from the University of Leeds and has co-founded the Blu Flamingo digital agency which now operates in four African countries.

Unexpected twists and turns

I came to my job as a reporter and a presenter quite by accident. I started out as an artist, having done an art degree at university, majoring in watercolour painting and anatomy drawing. Never did I think I would end up as a journalist or at the BBC.

I was born in Tanzania and grew up in Uganda, where I pretty much thought I would stay for the rest of my life. But I took opportunities that came up. My parents didn't have a lot, and I was only able to go to university because I got a scholarship from the government. So that was good, but I still had to work three jobs while studying. People talk about how fun university was, but it wasn't for me! But we all have different experiences. I had a graphic design job, which I did during the week, and I did a weekend show on the radio.

> *"I grew up with a very practical mindset – basically in a survival mode. I wasn't thinking about what would make me happy, what I enjoyed – there were bills to be paid. It wasn't until later that I taught myself to listen to myself about what I wanted."*

Because of that, I got a TV opportunity. Someone heard me on the radio and suggested I applied for an opening. I thought it wasn't for me – I had braces, I was really pimply, and only perfect people did TV. If it weren't for my sister, who said I should do it, I probably wouldn't have gone for it. But I did the interview, they gave me a shot and that's how I ended up in the newsroom. I did some TV reporting and eventually an opportunity opened up in Kenya. It was while I was in Kenya that I won the BBC Komla Dumor Award for African journalists, which came with a three-month secondment to London. So I came to London very much with the attitude that, yes, this was about me learning from the BBC, but it was also about the BBC learning from me. The African audience is very big. There were ways I felt the BBC could improve its coverage of Africa, and I was very vocal about that. Thankfully, the BBC was very receptive to my ideas. I stayed after that and I'm still here.

Understanding yourself

I think we often give too much prominence to people's backgrounds. They play a part, but they're not the sum of who we are. But I think they do shape you in some ways. I grew up with a very practical mindset – basically in a survival mode. I wasn't thinking about what would make me happy, what I enjoyed – there were bills to be paid. It wasn't until later that I taught myself to listen to myself about what I wanted. Even with small things like buying a kettle – of course, it needs to be practical, it needs to last a long time and do the job it's supposed to do. But then I had to teach myself that I could also just buy something I liked, and if it broke after three months, I could get another one. Also, did it make me happy? Did I like the way it looked?

Rediscovering yourself

A lot of my journey of discovering who I am was about going back to who I was as a child, before all the difficult things in life. I remembered that I liked to read and I liked to write, and I have memories of playing teacher and doing a roll call of my stuffed animals because I liked to teach. There is an element of teaching in journalism in that you're learning information and passing it on. So I think the journey for me

> *"I think it's really important to focus not on what we think that role is, but who we are, and what we want to bring to that situation."*

was a process of remembering those parts of who I was, rather than becoming something else. And I don't think it was a moment, but a series of events that encouraged me to become more of myself, of who I really am.

Speaking out

Through my TV career, especially when I went to Kenya, there have been policies about how you dress. In Kenya, I had a fight with the management about my hair, because I've always worn my hair natural but they wanted me to straighten it or wear a weave. There's nothing wrong with that, but it just wasn't me. So I had to speak out and say I didn't feel comfortable and wouldn't be able to be myself on set, which would come across to the viewers. It was difficult because I'd just got there and it wasn't the time to be ruffling feathers. But looking back, I'm very glad I did. I feel like it did change things and make it easier for the people who did come after me to wear their hair however they wanted.

Redefining opportunities

Sometimes I think we cancel ourselves out of roles because we don't see ourselves in how we perceive that role. In Kenya, TV is a big national event, and I was thrust into a world where all the news anchors were big celebrities. Although I was in leadership positions at school, I'm very much an introvert and I like to spend time by myself. I need time to recharge before I get back into the public eye. So a lot of my personality was at odds with how I saw journalists to be. I'm bubbly and effervescent, but I didn't feel like any of those things. I think it's really important to focus not on what we think that role is, but who we are, and what we want to bring to that situation.

I realized that I may not be super-talkative and the life and soul of the party, but I'm a really good listener. That's an excellent skill for a journalist so I try to focus on interviews and taking time with people to get to know them and understand their lives. I care very deeply about the people whose stories I report on, and I'd like to think that comes through in my reporting. So I focus on that as a strength rather than things I don't have.

Replacing the fear

Even though I'd moved from Uganda to Kenya, that was only a hop step away. It was an hour's flight, and I was still in Africa. But moving to the UK, so far away from family and friends – that was definitely scary. I didn't know how it was going to turn out. My entire education had been in Africa. I didn't know whether I would fit in somewhere like the BBC. People there had gone to certain schools and had a

"Sometimes I think we cancel ourselves out of roles because we don't see ourselves in how we perceive that role."

certain understanding of the world that maybe I didn't have. And that was scary. But in terms of overcoming fear, I think nature abhors a vacuum. You can't really get rid of fear – you have to replace it with something else. So I focused on what I could do for the stories about Africa at the BBC, where that message needs to be heard even more than at home. I tried to focus on that rather than on what I was afraid of.

ADE ADEPITAN

Ade Adepitan MBE is a TV presenter, paralympic medalist, journalist, and father. Born in Lagos, Nigeria and raised in East London, Ade survived polio as a youngster. Ade went on to succeed as an international Paralympic wheelchair basketball player and renowned broadcaster. Ade's work has taken him across the globe; going undercover with C4's, *Dispatches*, reporting foreign affairs for *Unreported World*, and more recently fronting the ground-breaking BBC Two series *Climate Change: Ade on the Frontline*.

Q So my first question is, who is Ade? And how did you get to know yourself?

A Who is Ade? Ade is many things. I've evolved over the years, as we all do. I'm a version of who I was all those years ago, but different layers get added as we experience new things. Young Ade was feisty with a big mouth. He was confident, naive, excited, determined – really, really determined. I grew up in the East End of London, and I went to a school where I was one of only three Black kids and a few Asian kids, and I was the only disabled child. So whether I liked it or not, I was always singled out as being different. I was always judged the moment people saw me because of the way I walked, because of my strong

Nigerian accent, and because I was Black. I had all of these things, which ended up making me resilient from an early age. Resilient and also I had to learn to find my voice early. Because when you're different, if you don't find your voice, people will decide who you are without even giving you a choice.

So that was me in the early days. A lot of my friends from where I grew up never left East London, but when I moved out and started meeting people from different backgrounds and walks of life, I became more open minded and interested in more things. Thanks to sport I was able to travel the world – and I think that's one of the greatest gifts that you can have. I'd always had this hunger, this wanderlust, to see the world and to meet different people. I left home when I was 17 so I had to find my own way from a really young age. Then, when I was 19, I moved to Spain. Now when I look at it, I think I was brave to go to a different country where I didn't speak the language, where I knew nobody. I lived in a youth hostel at first and then moved in with a Spanish family. I was the only Black person in that village and one of a only few disabled people. I played professional basketball for the local team, learned the language, and grew up. That time shaped who I am today. I understood more about being outside my comfort zone, and I learned to push and challenge myself.

> *"I understood more about being outside my comfort zone, and I learned to push and challenge myself."*

And then I got into TV, completely by luck. TV was never on my agenda. I never thought about being a TV presenter, mainly because I never saw anybody like myself on the box. I saw a few Black people on TV, but not many, and rarely any disabled people. And no one who was Black and disabled, so there was no blueprint, no one for me to aspire to be. But luckily for me, I met people who believed in me. And this is one thing I learned: you can't get anywhere on your own. You need your community, your tribe. You need people who believe in you more than you believe in yourself. People who can pick you up on those days when you're down and who can keep it real when your head is floating too high above the skies. At the time you might not appreciate their tough love, but in future years you'll probably be grateful.

I'm thankful for the people I met along the way, who made me more open and accepting of people who I didn't think I should have anything to do with because of where I'd come from. I got to where I am because of two middle-class white guys who spotted me. They were making a film for their cable TV channel and they did a video diary about me. They loved my attitude and the way it came across on camera, and they told me that I should be a TV presenter, and I was like, "Are you having a laugh?" I remember going back and telling friends and they said things like, "People like us don't get on TV. Look at your accent. Look at the way you talk. They'll laugh at you. TV is for posh people." And I believed my friends. But these guys opened doors for me, and before I knew it, I was presenting children's TV and then I got an agent. Never put any limitations on who you are and who you want to be. Don't allow the fear of failure to stop you from trying to achieve your dreams. If it scares you, if it makes you feel edgy, if you feel like you're being challenged, then it's a good thing.

Q Oh, that's amazing. Thank you so much, you've covered so many things. Are there any moments that you can think of when you had to put your foot down and really speak your mind?

A There are plenty of times I've had to speak up for myself. Something people don't always appreciate is that when you have a disability, you really have to struggle to have control of your life. Everybody wants to tell you how you should you live, what you should do, what's safe for you to do, what you can't do. So I've always fought for my right to do the things that I believe in. I don't know where that came from, probably my parents.

So on my first day of school, I wanted to play football with the other kids, but they thought that I'd be no good because of the way I walked. I had to fight tooth and nail to convince them and show them, through my actions, what I was capable of.

"Never put any limitations on who you are and who you want to be. Don't allow the fear of failure to stop you from trying to achieve your dreams. If it scares you, if it makes you feel edgy, if you feel like you're being challenged, then it's a good thing."

Another big moment for me speaking up was while I was presenting a TV series called *The Holiday Programme*. In the late 1990s and early 2000s, people weren't used to seeing someone like me on TV. As a straight-talking East Londoner, I'm quite colloquial in the way I talk, but I think

> **"I had to fight tooth and nail to convince them and show them, through my actions, what I was capable of."**

I'm a good communicator. It might not be the textbook way of someone who's been to university, but I think I can get across the message. The director I was working with had this mindset that he had to really script me – really put words into my mouth. The links they gave me weren't what I would say, weren't how I would explain things. I said that I could explain the stories – about this wine in the Dordogne or these beautiful horses in their special area of France, and all this cultured stuff, which they don't expect working class people to know about – but I'd do it in my way. We had this really high battle, and it was tough because I was in the early stages of my career and I had imposter syndrome, where I felt I shouldn't even be there. How was I qualified to be arguing with these people who had been in TV for a lot longer than me, and who'd been to university? I didn't have any of their grades, but I stuck to my guns. I met the director halfway and rejigged the script a bit. I said it partly my way and I fitted in some of his stuff. But when I came back to the UK, I went to see the head of the show with my agent, and I said, "Look, I'm not doing this show unless you let me do it as me. Unless you let me be Ade Adepitan." And that set the tone for me in my TV career onwards. I think sometimes you have to make a stand early, otherwise you get dragged along and blown in the wind, like a kite. And that leads to frustration and even mental illness because you no longer feel like yourself. The hardest thing in life, I feel, is trying to be someone else – trying to be something that other people want you to be. Carrying that facade is like carrying a heavy weight, and it wears you down eventually. So you have to fight to be you.

> *"The hardest thing in life, I feel, is trying to be someone else – trying to be something that other people want you to be."*

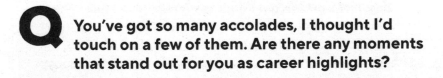 **You've got so many accolades, I thought I'd touch on a few of them. Are there any moments that stand out for you as career highlights?**

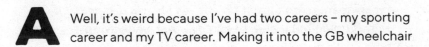 Well, it's weird because I've had two careers – my sporting career and my TV career. Making it into the GB wheelchair

basketball squad for the Sydney Paralympics in 2000 would be one of my highlights, simply because it was a really, really difficult journey for me. My parents were dead set against me playing sport. They wanted me to get AAA grades and go to university like a good Nigerian boy. I'm not stupid, but I think the way education was taught when I was growing up wasn't right for me.

My father and I weren't getting on. We patched things up later on, which was really important, but early on my father was adamant that I wouldn't play sport. When I was 17, I was the British powerlifting champion and I'd been selected for the junior squad for the World Championships. I was also in a senior wheelchair basketball team and was knocking on the door of the junior Great Britain team. So I had all of these opportunities in sport right in front of me, and sport is something that I really love doing. It really felt like what I was meant to do at that time in my life, but I knew I wasn't going to be able to achieve that while living at home with my parents.

I left home at 17. I didn't have much money, I didn't know how to cook, I didn't know how to run my house or anything like that, but somehow I found a way to get my life straight, to train enough, and to deal with the setbacks from not making it into the GB squad. I was turned down seven or eight times before I was finally selected. I started trying to get into the GB squad when I was 18, and I wasn't selected until I was 27. And that was a lonely period. I had so much self-doubt, I had to fend for myself, and I had to find a way on my own. But I look back now, and I admire what I was able to do.

"I was turned down seven or eight times before I was finally selected. I started trying to get into the GB squad when I was 18, and I wasn't selected until I was 27. And that was a lonely period."

So making it onto the squad in 2000 was definitely a big achievement for me. And then being part of the team that brought the Paralympics and the Olympics to London in 2012 was huge. As one of the sport ambassadors, I got to go out to Singapore with the team pitching the bid for London to be host city, and then later on I got to help shape Channel 4's coverage.

BAFTA award winning, wasn't it?

Yeah, Channel 4 had the philosophy that they really wanted to take the Paralympics coverage to another level. I can talk about being a part of that as a throwaway thing, but actually, to go from where I began to there was bonkers. When I stop and think about it, I was this kid born in Lagos, Nigeria. I had a disability, my older sister got a disability, and my parents came from a really impoverished background. We came to the UK in the 1970s and we struggled and we struggled and we struggled. I didn't go to university, but then somehow I find myself presenting the Paralympics in 2012 with Claire Balding. It's nuts.

Then, I guess, my next big achievement was getting my first series with my name on it – *Africa with Ade Adepitan* on BBC Two. I pinch myself. I still can't believe that I was able to do these things and have a career in TV for more than 20 years.

So was there a time when you drew strength to overcome something you were scared of?

This is a story I've never told. It's quite a hard story. When we were at school, my friends and I used to go out to get lunch. There was me – a Black African kid, a West Indian, and a Pakistani. And when we were 13, we were subjected to a racial attack. We were going for chip butties, and these kids just jumped us and it was bad. They were bigger and older than us, about 15 or 16, and there were more of them. My Pakistani friend got beaten so badly you couldn't see his face because of the blood. It was so awful and so horrific, and what was really hard for us was that people stood around and watched and didn't do anything – maybe out of fear. I don't think any of us really recovered properly from that.

After that, I swore to myself that I'd never stand by if something like that happened again – that I'd never allow fear like that to destroy the life of me or my friends or anyone that I cared about. It still haunts me. I wished I'd done something, but there probably wasn't anything I could have done. They were so big and there were so many of them. I don't want to be in that position ever again. It's super scary.

Q **What would you say to young Ade? Any words of advice?**

A I would say, don't ever put a limitation on what you can achieve. And don't allow the judgements of others or their parameters be your limit.

"*I think sometimes you have to make a stand early, otherwise you get dragged along and blown in the wind, like a kite.*"

ADE ADEPITAN

"I learned from other people about things on set, so if someone can learn from me about how to be more inclusive and make the environment more accessible on their next job, then that's when I can lend my voice for positive change."

RUTH MADELEY

"In my 20s, I really wasn't that good at fully being myself."

GREG JAMES

"When you're different, if you don't find your voice, people will decide who you are without even giving you a choice."

ADE ADEPITAN

INTERVIEW WITH

GREG JAMES

Greg James is an award-winning radio/TV presenter and writer. He currently presents BBC Radio 1's Breakfast Show and co-hosts the BBC 5 Live podcast, *Tailenders*, with Felix White and Jimmy Anderson. His most renowed writing project was the creation of the children's book *Kid Normal* (co-written with Chris Smith), released in July 2017, which topped the children's books charts. The pair have since written five more in the series and recently released their latest best-selling venture, *The Great Dream Robbery*.

Q **Can you paint a picture of what young Greg was like? And then how you got to know yourself?**

A Well, it's a big subject, isn't it? But it's something I've been thinking about a lot recently. Maybe because of my age, maybe because of the pandemic, but I've been taking stock and asking, "Where am I? Where was I? How did I get here? And what do I want to do with the rest of my life?" Weirdly, in the last few years – probably since taking over *Radio 1 Breakfast* – I feel like I've returned to being nearer to

> **"It's about having the confidence to shout about the things that you really like."**

my 11- or 12-year-old self. I guess it's about having the confidence to shout about the things that you really like, that you're passionate about and, that you're knowledgeable about. In my 20s, I really wasn't that good at fully being myself. I'll be forever grateful for being on Radio 1 from the age of 21. It's been a really interesting 15 years where I've tried stuff out, but I've found that essentially, I've always been the same.

Young me was kind of like me now, because I really loved silly things and making people laugh with funny voices and falling over and that kind of thing. But also, I was quite shy. I wasn't the loudest person at school or the most confident. I really hated speaking in class and I still don't really like being centre of attention, which is quite odd, I suppose, considering the job I now do presenting on the radio.

As a kid, I was just really happy. My mum was a PE teacher, and she did a lot of sport with me. We had a really nice time together doing athletics and lots of running, cricket, and football. My dad and I would make stuff together. I loved to make funny videos and I tried to copy things I'd seen on Saturday night TV, like making a gladiators' assault course.

And I was really obsessed with special effects like smoke machines and strobe lights and lasers. I bought a cheap disco ball to make special effects on my videos. Once I made a body double of myself and threw it out the window to recreate a stunt I'd seen in a film where someone jumped from a burning building. Much to the horror of my mum!

"Before you can communicate who you are, first you have to find it out for yourself."

With my friends, I'd record little radio shows, so I've always been into that type of thing. At one point, I really wanted to be a camera operator. I remember seeing on TV one of those cameras that slides across the floor. I was like, "Oh my God, that's the coolest thing ever! A camera that zooms around the floor!" Our video camera had a tripod and I put dusters on the bottom of its feet so it would slide across the kitchen lino. I really loved all that sort of thing, but I never shared those nerdy little passions with people.

Sport was a big part of my childhood. I really enjoyed cricket and being in the team gave me confidence. And I was into anything that moves: remote control cars, model cars, model planes. So I always liked little gadgets, which is good because when you're on the radio, you're messing around with gadgets the whole time.

As I said, I wasn't the most confident person, but I would always try to make my friends at school laugh by copying funny bits from films, like being Jim Carrey or Austin Powers. I definitely liked clowning around.

My main bit of advice for anyone who wants to do a similar type of job – one that requires you to put your personality out there – is to be patient. Before you can communicate who you are, first you have to find it out for yourself. And that took me a long time. I mean, I've always been myself and there's always been bits of me on the radio. But inevitably, when you're in your 20s, you're finding out about your personality and you're working out your passions, your beliefs, your political stance, and where you stand on certain issues. And it was quite weird for me to do all that publicly.

To go on the radio, as well as being that person we know in real life, you've got to be funny and find a good punch line and you've got to know all about the music and be good at interviewing, and all that takes time. So patience is really crucial. I think you just have to be ready for things whenever you're ready. And if you miss out on something, it's actually for a reason. I didn't get the breakfast show when Nick Grimshaw got it because I wasn't ready. I wasn't a fully formed person, and I hadn't quite nailed who I was on the radio. But when the opportunity came along in 2018, I was in a better place. I'd done some soul-searching, I'd made some mistakes, I'd had some terrible and some great relationships, I'd had some bad times and some great times on the radio. And then, things slotted into place.

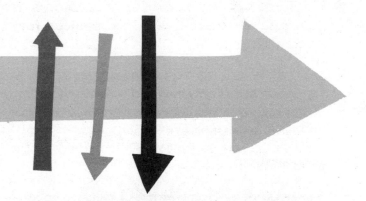

It's easy to get lost in thinking, "Oh, my God, I'm a radio DJ, what does that mean? It means that now I have to like this certain thing and do that certain thing. And I don't talk about nerdy things any more, like gardening or how much I love cricket." But of course, you should. Those are the things that make you who you are. They might not be relatable to every person on earth, but nothing is. That's why stations like the ones we have at the BBC are so great because they allow you to be an actual person. You're allowed to go on your show and say your opinions – not political ones, obviously – but you can have your say on other things. And talk about what you did at the weekend. As long as you can make that relatable in some way to the listeners, they'll find it interesting. Because everyone's got passions – those things that they're like, "Oh, I don't know if it's the coolest thing, but I do like it."

I feel so much happier being myself on the radio now than I did, even five or six years ago. It feels like I'm not doing as much of an act as I used to do.

 Have you got any examples that come to mind of a time when you've had to speak up for yourself?

 I guess there have been lessons for me about backing myself. Moments when you think, "You know what, I deserve to be here. And all this stuff in my head is just a narrative I've created. I'm going to show everyone that actually I can do this."

But that's not really an example of speaking up for yourself. I have a very privileged life – that's the problem with asking someone like me that question because I'm not ignored very often. It's lucky for me, but it's a horrible state of affairs. I'm always allowed to have a say because I'm a middle-class white guy.

I don't have those moments where I feel I have to go, "Hang on a minute. That's unfair on me," because I think everyone's been very fair to me. I guess that's my truthful answer.

Q **Have you ever had any moments where everything's been against how you're feeling? When you've listened to your gut?**

A Yeah, loads of times. I mean, the whole reason I'm still on Radio 1 is because, whenever my mind doubts myself, my gut just goes, "No, you've got this. You can do this." I do overanalyze everything, all the time. I'm constantly self-therapizing myself: "Am I enjoying this? I'm enjoying this. Good. But, am I okay, here? Do I want to do this tomorrow?" I've broken my life and my career down into much smaller pieces, day by day, really. So, I do go with my gut quite often.

Jumping into writing children's books was something where I thought, "Do I want to? Can I do this?" My instinct was that I'd always wanted to write and commit something to paper, so I thought, "I can do this." So you've just got to have the courage of your convictions and throw yourself into it.

So I do listen to my gut a lot. And it's often right. To be honest with you, I did have a chat with my boss this time last year, to say that I wasn't sure how much more I could do *Radio 1 Breakfast* in the pandemic. I wasn't really sure I was doing the right thing anymore. I didn't know whether I was being any good at it any more. I didn't know if I could summon up the energy. I was worried about all my family and friends and loved ones. She told me to go away in the summer and have some time. I did some soul-searching. My brain was going mad, but my gut was saying that I still had lots more to do. I learned that it was really important to have that conversation and say, "Actually, I'm struggling a bit here." I needed to at least vocalize that, even if it meant that what I was saying was nonsense. And it turned out that it was nonsense. It was my brain being tired and emotional and confused.

"So you've just got to have the courage of your convictions and throw yourself into it."

I spoke my boss more recently, and she said she knew I wasn't actually going to leave at that point. But the conversation helped our relationship. She got to know me a bit better. I'm still learning, but it's really good to be honest about your feelings. Even a dream job can be hard. And when you're juggling your actual life, it's okay to change your mind. People say to go with your gut, but sometimes you don't know what that is. So you can change your mind.

> *"I do tend to obsess over certain decisions, but I'm trying to get out of the habit of overthinking."*

Also, I think that, whatever your decision, it was right in that moment. You might look back and think it wasn't right, but that's okay, because you're doing something else now. And you can learn from it.

When I was a kid, I thought that all adults knew their decisions were right every single time. And that's not true. Because I'm an adult. And I make decisions sometimes and I go, "Oh, yeah, I could have done the other thing, and it would have been fine." Or, "Maybe I should have done the other thing." There will be decisions in your life that you will look back on and go, "Hey, I could have gone the other way." Hopefully you don't regret them, but there will always be something else that comes along. I do believe that.

If you're determined and you're working hard and you're doing the right things, then other things will come up. I do tend to obsess over certain decisions, but I'm trying to get out of the habit of overthinking.

Q **Has there been any time that you felt fearful about something? And how did you overcome it?**

A That's a really good question. It's probably doing my job, which can be quite scary if you overthink it. I always wanted to do *Radio 1 Breakfast*, but I was terrified of it. I think I'm one of those people who quite thrives off a bit of fear. Weirdly, I sort of dread everything I'm about to do, like starting the breakfast show. As soon as I said, "Yes, I want to do it," I immediately went, "Oh, God, I've got to actually do it now."

"I think I'm one of those people who quite thrives off a bit of fear."

But I think dreading things makes me better at them because I really concentrate, though that's probably an unhealthy way to live anxiety-wise. Before that first show, I was like, "Can I do this? Am I going to be able to do it?" Then, after that first show, or even after the first 10 minutes, I thought, "Oh my God, I can do it. I'm doing it! Look, look, look, mum. I'm doing it without stabilizers!" It was like riding my bike merrily through the park being like, "Yeah, I'm doing it!"

I don't think I was scared of it so much as full of self-doubt. But that's probably healthy. If you're walking around thinking that you can just nail everything, then you're an absolute clown. I think the honest way to approach stuff is to think, "I think I can do that. It's going to be hard, but I'll try my very best." I always make sure that I prepare properly. No one can just swan into any job and do it. So it's more like the fear of not doing something well that I have to get over. And actually, I get this huge sense of relief when I record a radio show. I do a few shows on Radio 4 and when I walk in there, I think, "Oh my God, today I might do a terrible show." Then at the end of it, I go, "Oh, phew. I didn't." But that's only because I've put the hours in to make it good. That fear of failure spurs me on and drives me to do good things.

■ ■■ ■■ ■■ ■ ■ ■ ■ ■■ ■■ ■ ■

"I think the honest way to approach stuff is to think, "I think I can do that. It's going to be hard, but I'll try my very best."

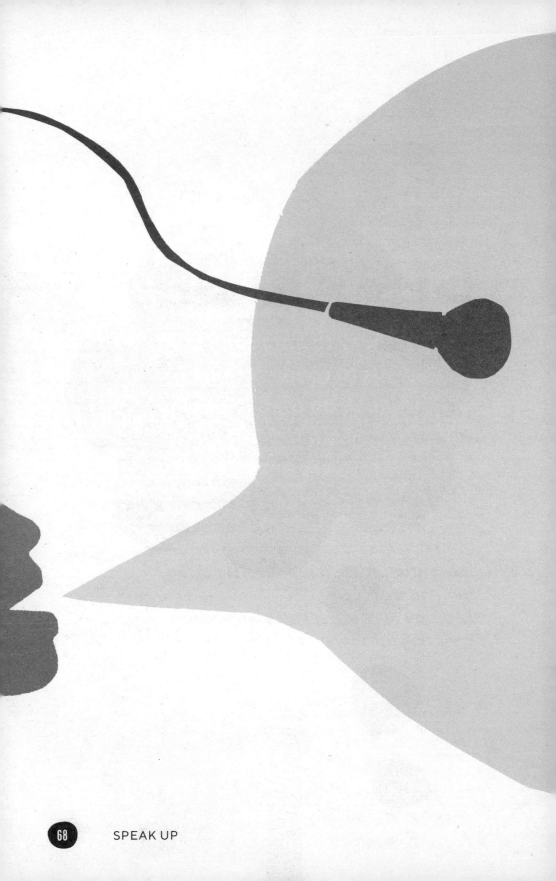

SPEAK UP

2

SPEAK UP

Speaking up comes naturally to me, but so many of us are afraid, worried, or simply don't believe in it. Whatever the situation, whether your food order is incorrect, or you have witnessed something that requires someone in authority, even when you need to defend yourself amongst your siblings, being able to say what you feel can be challenging. But, there are ways to express yourself, and some are non-verbal (holding silence can also be impactful!) Try to find a time, place, and method that feels right for you. And it may help you to know just how empowering speaking up has been for other people.

INTERVIEW WITH

JJ CHALMERS

JJ Chalmers' career as a Royal Marines Commando was cut short after he suffered life-changing injuries following an IED explosion in Afghanistan. After years of rehabilitation, JJ went on to compete in the 2014 Invictus Games where he captained the Trike Cycling team and won three medals. JJ took on a studio presenter role in 2016 for the Rio Paralympics, and since 2017 has anchored BBC1's coverage of the Invictus Games. JJ has become a key part of the BBC's sports team with highlights including The Commonwealth Games and The London Marathon.

A life-changing moment

Ten years ago I was a Royal Marines Commando, though that seems like a whole other life ago. And in some ways it was – I feel like I was reborn on the 27th of May 2011. I was serving in Helmand Province in Afghanistan, operating on the front line of a war zone in a really complex place. I was in a team of about ten guys and we had to search a bomb-making factory. Our big threat in Afghanistan at the time was improvised explosive devices (IEDs) – homemade landmines. The media often calls them roadside bombs. One of the guys on my team stepped on one of these. I was having a conversation with him when the blast went off, and the blast wave bludgeoned me from head to toe. My life and limbs were saved by the 19 and 20-year-old guys who got me to a helicopter. The next thing I knew, I was waking up in Birmingham, a week later.

I opened my eyes and had to start all over again. I had to be physically rebuilt and then relearn how to use my body, how to walk again, how to feed myself, how to do all the things that a kid has to do. Also, my career was over. I had to start again there, too. It was life changing, and in some ways, it was life ending. But a new life starts again. Having said that, there are parts of my old life that still influence who I am today.

Where it all began

I joined the Royal Marines when I was 17. I'd been a cadet when I was at school so I'd had some insight into that world. There were lots of reasons why I joined, but the simplest one is that I wanted a life of service. I'd been raised in a house where you do something for the greater good: my brother's a teacher; my sister's a nurse; my dad's a minister. We come from an environment where you're part of a bigger machine, and you contribute in some way. Service comes in different shapes and forms, but joining the Royal Marines was my way to give something back. But actually, I was getting something out of it as well because it was a challenge that I wanted to see if I could accomplish.

"I had to be physically rebuilt and then relearn how to use my body, how to walk again, how to feed myself, how to do all the things that a kid has to do."

Aiming high

The guys who wore green berets were super heroes to me. It seemed impossible that I could become one of them. I'd never really done anything in my life that seemed impossible. But if they could do it, maybe I could? So I started down that path. It was really tough, but I was motivated to become a Marine Commando – to join the greatest club on earth and be part of a brotherhood.

This was the early 2000s so the Marines had been on operations in Iraq and Afghanistan, but also on peacekeeping and disaster-relief operations – some pretty extraordinary things. From the way they talked about it, you realized that they'd been through hardships and good times but the important thing was that they'd been through everything together. And that was what really hooked me – the idea of having guys like that in your corner. Being part of a really special club. That idea has looked after me during the toughest things I've faced. It shapes who you are as a person and fills you with important values like selflessness, courage, and determination – probably more than adversity does. The other thing is, as hard as being a Marine was, it was also pretty good fun. It was amazing to make the extraordinary pretty ordinary. And I say that now, looking back at it 10 years later.

Of course, there were some really miserable times, and I'm not talking about getting blown up. I mean being cold, wet, and miserable most of the time. But actually, I pinch myself when I think about the things I used to do: jumping out of helicopters, storming buildings – the stuff you see in movies. That was my job. But I'm so far removed from that life now that I can't quite believe I did it.

"The guys who wore green berets were super heroes to me. It seemed impossible that I could become one of them. I'd never really done anything in my life that seemed impossible. But if they could do it, maybe I could?"

Starting again

After the explosion, I was in hospital for nine weeks, but I was far from fixed at that point. They had rebuilt my body, but I was still massively dependent on other people and a huge level of medication. I couldn't drive my car; I couldn't feed myself properly; I struggled to get my clothes on in the morning. It was pretty miserable, but I realized quickly that I was lucky to be alive and I wasn't, for one second, going to feel sorry for myself. Particularly because a couple of my friends had lost their lives in that incident. So I had no choice but to get better. Also, being in a hospital, as wonderful as the care they give you is, it's not a nice place to be. I needed to get myself as far away as I could, which meant doing whatever I was told to get better.

Finding strength

After the hospital, I went to a place called Headley Court, which was the main rehabilitation facility for wounded, injured, and sick service personnel. I was in and out of that place for a year. Again, it was really tough, physically and mentally. But I do have some happy memories from that place because I was surrounded by guys and girls who were going through the same thing. Many of us had been blown up, though there's no blueprint for disability, and everybody has their own unique needs.

In some ways, it was hard because we weren't used to things being about us – we were the ones who helped other people. But being the one who was looked after was made easier by the fact that other people were going through it, too. Also, I saw guys and girls who'd been injured a few years earlier and been told they would never walk again, but who were now starting to run marathons, do Ironman triathlons, climb Everest, and row the Atlantic. Being around such extraordinary people, with such energy for getting better and proving something to themselves, helped me to jump through the hoops, go through rehab, and have more surgery. It was two steps forward, three steps back, then a few more forward. The journey was never in a single direction, and the path certainly wasn't straight, but I always knew that I'd get there in the end – even though I didn't know where "there" was.

Building resilience

Another thing that helps is perspective. I think people often struggle because we don't take pride in the little victories that happen every day. But when you adapt to a challenge this big, you realize that these small wins are enough. If I compared my achievements to what I used to be able to do, then my heart would break every single day. There's nothing great about a

Royal Marines Commando being able to put on a T-shirt or tie his shoelaces. But if I just looked at what I'd been able to do the day before, well, I was slightly further down the road. Though, of course, maybe the next day, I wouldn't be able to tie my shoelaces because I'd had more surgery. But knowing I could always get better and move forward was key. It's about finding which direction you're pointing in and taking small steps to get there. And not being disheartened by the fact that this huge mountain seems impossible to climb. In fact, I wasn't trying to climb a huge mountain – I was just trying to get up to the next rock.

I thought that if I could do this, then I could pretty much do anything. In fairness, the Marines had taught me that when I was 17, and they did it by throwing me in puddles and making me crawl through tunnels. Again, it was in those tough moments that I thought, "Okay, do I quit now? Or do I carry on, to get to where I want to be?" That resilience was in me, but it was heightened and improved. The thing about my recovery is that I really didn't have much choice: no way was I going to quit. I just had to keep going. But that's not to say that I felt like that every single day or every single hour. Of course, there were really tough moments along the way.

Looking forward

I did not know what I was going to do with my life, but I thought it would be okay. That is probably because I borrowed strength from those around me. I was lucky to have a good support network with my family, my friends, and my amazing girlfriend, who is now my wife. On my down days, I knew that they had my back.

Also, I could look at the experiences I was living through, and those I had lived through, and think, "Well actually, I've not wasted all my years up to now. Yes, my career's over, but being in the Marines wasn't a waste of time. I've learned so much and I've gained confidence and skills and qualifications. I'll be okay." But the most difficult thing was finding something as good as being a Royal Marine. I'd achieved my dream at the age of 18 and I'd lived it. So what was the new dream?

"Knowing I could always get better and move forward was key. It's about finding which direction you're pointing in and taking small steps to get there."

Making the most of opportunities

Then the Invictus Games came along. When I first heard about them, they didn't even have a name – we were just told that Prince Harry was putting on a sports competition for wounded, injured, and sick servicemen and women. We thought it would just be like a sports day, but we all signed up to it anyway because we were competitive. We liked our fitness and we wanted to get outside and break up our mundane recovery. I spent my life doing exercises like moving marbles from one tray to another. How do you make that more exciting? Well, you make it competitive, and you take it to a bigger stage. I started cycling and running, and when the Invictus Games happened in 2014 they weren't just a sports day. They were at the Olympic Stadium in London with banners, flashing lights, and TV cameras. It was like being a rock star for a week; like nothing I've ever experienced in my life. The games were televised by the BBC, and it was the first time I'd ever seen TV cameras.

Finding a new voice

One of the things Prince Harry said was that the Invictus Games were about something bigger than us. They were our recovery tool, of course, to help make us better physically, mentally, even socially. But Prince Harry said that they were also for people outside, looking in – people who'd never had an interaction with the military or with disability. It was an opportunity for us to inspire them as well as each other and to teach them about disability by being brutally honest and telling our stories. I really signed up to that idea. It all culminated when I won my medal in my cycling and was taken to the studio to be interviewed live on BBC One by Jonathan Edwards. They started pointing cameras at me, and I started talking.

"Prince Harry said that they were also for people outside, looking in – people who'd never had an interaction with the military or with disability. It was an opportunity for us to inspire them as well as each other and to teach them about disability by being brutally honest and telling our stories."

Putting myself out there

I was quite comfortable in the TV studio. Strangely, I was enjoying myself. I looked across at Jonathan Edwards (former triple jumper and BBC sports presenter), and he was doing an extraordinary job. He was presenting a live programme, and I could see straight away that he had a lot of plates spinning. Having done a complex job in the military, I'm used to lots of things going on at once and I like a challenge. So I could appreciate how much he was doing: reading and checking his scripts, keeping his eye on the basketball score, checking the autocue, making sure we were on time. A dozen things at once,

plus making me comfortable in this weird environment. All this, and he still had a smile on his face. I thought to myself, "That's what I want to do." So all of a sudden I asked, "Jonathan, how do I do this? How do I sit in your chair next time we do an interview?" He introduced me to a few people, I spoke to producers, and then a few people gave me a shot. And that's what got me into this industry.

I had discovered the thing that was going to get me out of bed in the morning. For me, the Invictus Games weren't just about sport and winning medals, they were about regaining the confidence and ambition to take me on to the next thing because, once the Games are over on Monday morning, who are you going to be? So, kind of foolishly, I decided that I'd become JJ Chalmers: broadcaster and TV presenter.

Why wouldn't it be you?

The TV and radio presenter Greg James played an important moment in the early part of my career. A few months after the Invictus Games, when I was thinking of getting into telly, we were both at the Wimbledon tennis tournament. We were having a wee chat, and I'll always remember what he said to me about that point when you think to yourself, "Well, this will never be me", and you give up. He said that you've just got to wake up in the morning and ask yourself why it wouldn't be you. Then, if you can figure out why, fix that problem. But actually, there's probably no reason why it shouldn't be you – you're just thinking that someone else is better, and that's probably not the case. So you should go out there and go for it. And that was a real moment for me thinking, "Yeah, I should just go for it."

> *"First and foremost, I'm a presenter, but I'm also a presenter with a disability, and I try to own that."*

Raising a voice for disability

It's an amazing privilege to make telly and radio, and I'm not one to take that lightly. I was always taught, not just in the Marines, but from a young age, to leave things in a better place than I found them. That's what I tried to do in Afghanistan and what I try to do in my life. I realize that the platform I have now comes with a responsibility, and I want to use it.

One of the most wonderful things about where I think the BBC is, and where society is moving, is a sense of genuine representation – rather than just a "let's tick some boxes" exercise. First and foremost, I'm a presenter, but I'm also a presenter with a disability, and I try to own that. I might be active, but there's no denying that there are things in my life where I need adjustments. It's really important that people who have a disability – which is, according to Scope, 9% of children, 21% of working age adults, and 42% of pension age adults in the UK – don't just see themselves, but hear and have their views represented. And that makes me really proud.

Of course, I've made programmes focused on disability like the Paralympics and the Invictus Games, and it's really important to have a knowledgeable voice that sits around those things. But to be the first presenter with a disability to present the Olympics both is and isn't something. It shouldn't be a big deal because it shouldn't be a big deal – it should just be the done thing. But then again, it is a big deal because there's some kid at home thinking to themselves, "Okay, I could do that".

I also like the moments of incidental disability. If a news story comes up on *The One Show* that involves disability, then I'm there with a real voice to talk about it. I always remember seeing Jermaine Jenas presenting *The One Show* the day after the Euros final, when young Black footballers had been racially abused. Who better to present your programme than a young black footballer? And he wasn't wheeled in specially to talk about it; he was there anyway. That's why representation is so important.

We've had a huge step forward with disability. Look at Rose Ayling-Ellis winning *Strictly Come Dancing*. That's incredible, but then again, she's one person in a cast of 30. Do 15% of the line-up and people working behind the cameras have a disability? Probably not. So can more be done? Absolutely. But are we moving in the right direction? Yes. And do I want to use my energy, knowledge and platform to move us that way? Absolutely.

"It's really important that people who have a disability... don't just see themselves, but hear themselves and have their views represented. And that makes me really proud."

GEORGE THE POET

George the Poet is a London-born spoken word performer of Ugandan heritage. His poetry has won him critical acclaim both as a recording artist and a social commentator. In the summer of 2018, he opened the wedding of Prince Harry and Meghan Markle with his poem "The Beauty of Union", and in 2019, his audio offering, the "Have You Heard George's Podcast?" won a prestigious Peabody Award and five Gold British Podcast Awards. George is now embarking on a PhD.

Q **How did you get into poetry?**

A It never occurred to me that I would be a poet. I got into poetry from being a rapper from the age of 15 – technically I was an MC in Grime. The Grime scene helped me to figure out how to put rhymes together, but what I really wanted was to comment on and respond to my environment. For me and my mates, the Grime scene was a space for us to express ourselves. That was very important, but I felt like there were some negative side effects to the way we were doing it, and poetry allowed me to deal with some of that. Rappers such as Chipmunk, Tinie, Tinchy, and N-Dubz were the commercial successes from my scene, but I had a different vision. I had a very critical mind, and I liked that about myself. I didn't want to have to keep dumbing it down and acting like I wasn't thinking about the things I was thinking about.

"For me and my mates, the Grime scene was a space for us to express ourselves."

Q You didn't want to just fit in?

A Exactly. In the early years, that's what I was doing – just rapping about rap. A bit about my environment, but not in a very critical way. Then, at 16, I started studying sociology. Wow – that's when it all came together. Because for the first time in school, we were talking about real life. I was in class, hearing all this stuff, and I knew that people back home would value hearing it in our language. And I could do that because I was in both worlds.

When I got to university, I was still thinking of myself as a rapper, but I was surrounded by people who were not from my background. That was cool, but made me realize that if I went on stage as a Grime MC, it wouldn't work. People wouldn't know what I was saying. And even if they did feel it, they wouldn't feel it how I intended. They used to see me as the cool Black guy. That was a gimmick, and it didn't give me space to speak about everything I wanted to speak about. So I decided to go on stage and just say what I had to say instead of performing it to a high-tempo Grime beat. I'd talk them through it like an essay. But I still used rhymes and wordplay and I still had passion so people started giving me the respect that I really wanted. And that let me know that I'd found my lane.

Q **You carved your own lane for yourself. It's amazing to see. Is there any moment when you had to dig deep, get brave, and go against the grain to use your voice for something that might have been uncomfortable?**

A Well, it started early on in my life. Before I was a rapper, I was a big brother. My little brothers used to play outside on the estate, and sometimes they'd get their bikes taken. As the big brother, I had to go and sort that out. So that's where I first really learned to stand up for my people. I think that was a very important experience.

> *"For the first time in school, we were talking about real life. I was in class, hearing all this stuff, and I knew that people back home would value hearing it in our language. And I could do that because I was in both worlds."*

Later on, I went to Cambridge University, which is a very different environment to where I grew up. I felt like I was representing people who were not there to speak for themselves, and I wasn't going to let anyone disrespect my people ever. From a young age, I felt there were problems that we were fuelling ourselves. In my early poetry career, I started criticizing some of the things I saw around me. And that was me standing up for my little brothers again. I was saying to the older guys of our community to stop recruiting our young people into the mistakes they'd made. Because, the beef will just perpetuate. They're young and they just want to belong to something. So I was criticizing my community, but I was also trying to represent us to people outside of our world. To let them know that we're proud, that we value ourselves, we love our area, we love the life and the culture that we come from. It's just that we've got some issues to work out.

And then highlighting these issues has carried on into my career. Now I talk a little more about Africa, and Uganda in particular. Sometimes it's not easy because I've got two sides of my life in Uganda – I've got street friends and I've got high-roller friends. Surprise, surprise, the high-rollers love the government, and the street ones feel the negative effects of the corruption and injustice. So when I speak on behalf of the street side, my high-roller friends get offended. They tell me I'm a Westerner misinterpreting their issues. But when I'm in the trenches, my friends there are really grateful that someone on this side of the world speaks so passionately for them.

Q Amazing. I want to ask you for a moment that stands out that you can celebrate. What's a highlight for you? A big win in your eyes that you've achieved?

A I would definitely say creating a life that someone else – that's my wife – wants to be part of. I'm married now and getting married has been the biggest event in my life up to this point. As a married man, I provide stability for another person. I provide a foundation for her to live her best life and be her full self.

Q That's an incredible achievement, to have that in your life. And I think it's nice to hear young men thinking about marriage as importantly as young women are told to.

A You're right. It's such a good point. In my podcast, I took a couple episodes out last season to talk about the process of getting married: what led to us deciding to do it and what it's like being in love. Because I realized that I never grew up with content like that. No one ever gave me a concept of what is to get married or spoke to me about a wedding or the cultural expectations. Like you said, boys are just not spoken to about this stuff, but it's very important.

Q **And you opened the royal wedding of Prince Harry and Meghan Markle with a poem of yours. I'm speechless – just by speaking your truth, you've been able to bless another union.**

A It's a real honour.

Q **Relating back to finding your voice, is there any advice that you would give young George the Poet? What would say to yourself?**

A Well, what I've learned to do is enjoy being present. Just enjoy the moment because you're never going to get it again, and usually what you need is right there. I think many of us find it helpful to have the right mentality when we need to create something from nothing. You need to assume that there's some advantage in your circumstance that you're going to use, or that is going to present itself to you, and everything's going to be alright. That's what ended up happening with my life, but when I was younger, I was stressing that it was never going to happen.

"So I was criticizing my community, but I was also trying to represent us to people outside of our world. To let them know that we're proud, that we value ourselves, we love our area, we love the life and the culture that we come from. It's just that we've got some issues to work out."

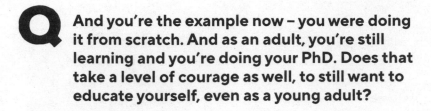

Q **And you're the example now – you were doing it from scratch. And as an adult, you're still learning and you're doing your PhD. Does that take a level of courage as well, to still want to educate yourself, even as a young adult?**

A Let me show you how deep it goes in my head. Hundreds of millions of years ago, there were dinosaurs, but these dinosaurs were around for more than a hundred million years – for way longer than we've been around. Humans started to come into the picture over the past 200,000 years or so. And society as we know it today has been in the making for a couple 1000 years. But as humans, we can only experience this whole timeline for maybe 100 years at a time. Maybe you'll be around for 100 years. So when you think about the potential that your contribution has to change the course of the the world, think about the fact that a group of people came up with the computer. And then some people discovered electricity, someone discovered light. It's just crazy – these new breakthroughs change everything. And that's how I see my journey.

So my to-do list for 2022 has to make sense in the grand scheme of things. Now, if I'm not really paying attention to where my information is coming from, or who I'm affecting, or how far my actions will reach, then I'm just not reaching my potential. But by paying a bit more attention to those things, you can have a real shot.

I was just speaking to my uncle. He came to the UK in the 1960s because, at the time, the Ugandan government was sending students abroad to get new skills and then come back and bless the country with what they'd learned. But then things changed back home and war broke out so he ended up staying here. And that made the whole backstory to my cousin growing up in the hood in London. These day-to-day decisions that we make affect people, basically forever. So my uncle was also advising me on marriage and saying pay attention to your wife, listen to her, respect her, talk everything through. If I take on his advice, I have a chance of building a family that's happy. We have to just continue to learn and pay attention to what's around us in order to live our best lives, not just for ourselves but for the people that we affect and for our legacy.

"Now, I think I'm comfortable at just throwing myself at anything really."

JJ CHALMERS

"We have to just continue to learn and pay attention to what's around us in order to live our best lives, not just for ourselves but for the people that we affect and for our legacy."

GEORGE THE POET

"I realized that we've only got one life, and mine was leaving me behind."

AMAR LATIF

"In the third year, I decided that enough was enough and I wasn't going to be wrapped up in cotton wool."

AMAR LATIF

"It was an opportunity for us to inspire them as well as each other and to teach them about disability by being brutally honest and telling our stories."

JJ CHALMERS

INTERVIEW WITH

AMAR LATIF

Amar Latif is a traveller, entrepreneur, and TV personality with an astonishing track record of facing up to major challenges. Due to an incurable eye condition, Amar lost 95% of his sight by the age of 19. In 2004, Amar founded Traveleyes, the world's first commercial tour operator to specialize in holidays for blind as well as sighted travellers. He has directed documentary films and appeared in a number of TV productions both as a presenter and actor.

Q Who was young Amar Latif? What was he like at school?

A Amar was a shy, confused little kid because when I was six, doctors broke the news to my parents that I was going to become blind in my middle-to-late teens. As I grew up, I was losing my sight. I started crashing into hurdles in sports and missing the ball in rugby. My desk got moved to the front of the class when I was about nine years old because I could no longer see the board from a distance. It was hard for me to fully engage with people around me because I was just trying to get by. So I wasn't really that confident.

But I used to love riding my bike and, to the horror of my mother, I still rode it up until the age of 16. One Sunday morning, my mum begged me not to go, but I thought I could see enough. I think I was getting tunnel vision so I could see a very narrow amount – parked cars to my left and a bit of the road to the right. So that morning, I went and crashed into this massive skip. I somersaulted and landed in the rubbish. There I was, somersaulting through the air, thinking, "Well, this should be the end of my cycling career."

I wasn't really that confident, but I did have a little bit of an entrepreneurial streak in me. I set up a tuck shop in my parents' house. I used to cycle to the cash-and-carry, bring a load of chocolates, set up my little stall and serve kids from the side window of the house. I loved doing that. So that was young Amar.

"As I grew up, I was losing my sight."

Q So, from going through that at such a young age, how was the transition between teenage and adult Amar to the job that you do you now?

A I remember I was 18 years old when I woke up and I couldn't see the poster at the end of my bed. I thought it was just morning fuzz so I closed my eyes and opened them up again. As I looked around the room, everything just was white. Like seeing cloud. That day I was walking around crashing into things, and I couldn't see the faces of my mum or dad or my brothers or sisters. I realized that I was blind. I remember thinking that I didn't want to be blind – I just wanted to go back to bed and wake up my normal self. But the reality was that my life had now changed forever.

So after many months of being depressed thinking I couldn't do anything and my parents saying I couldn't leave the house, I realized that we've only got one life, and mine was leaving me behind. I decided I might as well just get involved in things and see how it went because I had nothing to lose. I was blind anyway.

So with that approach, I went on to university. Teachers said that instead of studying maths and finance – what I wanted to do – I should study English and history because those subjects were easier for someone who's blind. But I was passionate about becoming an accountant. I think that's because when I was 12 years old, a girl in my class who I fancied wanted to be an accountant, so it was sexy. So I decided to do it anyway, and I actually got my degree in maths, stats, and finance.

While I was at uni, I remember walking around thinking that the other students were all having a great time. And here I was. And I felt quite depressed at moments. But then I just started taking things step by step and thinking innovatively. I recorded my textbooks and lecture notes onto cassettes, and things started to work. Then I actually got confident with it. In the third year, I decided that enough was enough and I wasn't going to be wrapped up in cotton wool and live in a protective box. So I headed off to Canada. And that created my armour of a new confidence. If you step outside your comfort zone, your world becomes bigger.

> *"That was my first time standing up for myself, and it gave me the confidence, I guess, over time to stand up for myself."*

Q Were there any moments that you can remember when you had to stand up for yourself? When you had to literally raise your voice and say, "I'm going to speak for myself here"?

A Well, the first time I found myself speaking up was when I was about 10 years old. I'd been moved to a school for blind children and two years later, they wanted me to go on to the next school for blind kids, but I didn't want to do that. I wanted to go to mainstream school. Back then, the teachers advised that the education I got would be much better if I went to a blind school, but I remember speaking up and saying to my dad that I wanted to be like everybody else. My father wanted to follow the teachers' advice, but I told him that I really didn't want to be segregated. That I knew I couldn't see and that my sight was going to get worse, but I just wanted to be "normal". So my dad fought my corner at the school meetings, and eventually I did go to mainstream school where they had support for visually impaired children on the side. And that was great. That was my first time standing up for myself, and it gave me the confidence, I guess, over time to stand up for myself.

Another time I used my voice was after I graduated from uni. I applied for so many jobs and went to interviews, but I kept getting rejected. All my sighted friends were landing great finance jobs with big salaries, and I didn't understand

> *"Hopefully that kind of discrimination is a thing of the past now, but at the time I used it as an impetus to do something about it and move my career forward."*

what was going on. Then one of the accountancy firms wrote to me saying that the reason why they didn't give me a job was because, although I seemed like a nice guy, they just didn't believe that a blind person could be an accountant. That came as a shock. Hopefully that kind of discrimination is a thing of the past now, but at the time I used it as an impetus to do something about it and move my career forward. So at the next interview I went to, I spoke up and said, "Excuse me, have you met a blind person before?" They said, "No", so I said, "Do you mind if I do a presentation for five minutes where I explain to you a little bit about blindness and about how, as a blind person, I would actually do the job?" And I gave them some successful blind role models of the time. They were fascinated with how I could do the job, and from that point onwards, I started to receive job offers. It taught me that obstacles don't always mean blocks in your path. They can be opportunities that can lead to incredible things as long as you have the right mindset.

Q You touched on listening to your gut when you spoke about not wanting to go to a blind school, but do you have any other examples?

A Yes, after working at British Telecom for seven years, I was heading up the commercial finance division. I loved my job and had a great salary. I had money and I wanted to travel the world, but when I approached travel companies I faced rejection. They wouldn't enable me to travel as an independent blind traveller. A lot of them said that I needed to bring somebody with me, and even if I did, I still wouldn't be able to go on the more adventurous holidays.
I thought that this was so unfair. Something in my gut was telling me that you only have one life, and if you want something that doesn't exist you either do without or you've got to build it yourself. So I decided to jump off the corporate cruise ship of employment and onto the dinghy of entrepreneurship – against the advice of my poor father, who had inspired me to get to this stage. He said, "Amar, I can't believe you're going to leave your well-paid job. You've always wanted to work for it." But inside my gut, I knew that I wanted to travel because these restrictions were making me feel like the world was closing in. I was starting to feel blind again. So in 2004, I set up Traveleyes – the world's first ever tour operator to take groups of blind and sighted people on holiday.

"Something in my gut was telling me that you only have one life, and if you want something that doesn't exist you either do without or you've got to build it yourself."

Q **Is there anything you have to say about overcoming fear? Was there ever a time when you were scared even though you were on your journey?**

A When I was young, I was always scared of heights and roller-coasters and stuff like that. My two sisters would always be so brave and jump on the roller-coasters, and I'd pretend that I had a sore stomach. But since losing my sight and having that mindset of throwing myself at whatever's out there, I've managed to just do those things. I go skydiving and bungee jumping. People say that it must help that I can't see, but you still know that you're high up. You can still sense it in an aeroplane when you're about to jump out the door. If you're jumping off a bridge, you know that you're jumping off a bridge. So now, I think I'm comfortable at just throwing myself at anything really. There is still one little thing that I'm still fearful about and need to overcome, and that's touching animals. Because I can't see how sharp their teeth are and stuff like that, I don't know where to stroke them and touch them.

Q What would you say to younger Amar to keep him inspired? Now you know how your life pans out, are there any words or little gems you would say to the younger you?

A I'd say, "Don't feel overwhelmed by the world. Take things step by step. Don't feel like you've got this big mountain to climb of challenges and problems. As long as you put one foot in front of the other, before long, you'll be up this mountain. And when you turn around and look, you'll see how beautiful the world really is."

"Obstacles don't always mean blocks in your path. They can be opportunities that can lead to incredible things as long as you have the right mindset."

"Inside my gut, I knew that I wanted to travel because these restrictions were making me feel like the world was closing in. I was starting to feel blind again."

"As long as you put one foot in front of the other, before long you'll be up this mountain."

LISTEN TO YOUR GUT

3

LISTEN TO YOUR GUT

When you finally know who you are and you can recognize the voice within, the next step is listening to it. The times you feel you should turn right instead of left, when you choose one course or job over another, even the clothes you decide to wear each day – are all examples of listening to your gut insincts. For me, feeling what is right, and trusting that feeling, has been life-changing. But I've also had experiences of not listening to my gut and, with hindsight, wishing I had. It's a learning curve – one that many of us are still on.

MOLLIE KING

During Mollie's time in the pop group The Saturdays, the group sold over 5 million records worldwide, achieving 13 Top 10 singles and 5 Top 10 albums. In 2018, Mollie turned her hand to presenting. She hosts the *Matt and Mollie* Radio 1 show with Matt Edmondson and her own Friday morning show *Best New Pop*. In addition to radio, Mollie has also guest-presented *This Morning*, she covered the entertainment slot on *Lorraine*, and has guest presented on *Blue Peter*. Mollie is a proud ambassador for the Dyslexia Association, an organization for people with a neurological difference Mollie was diagnosed with as a child.

Q **What was younger Molly like? What were you into? And how did that lead to what you're doing now?**

A Younger Mollie was very much the same as I am today – a massive dreamer. Growing up, I seemed to base my whole life around music. When I was younger, I found school really difficult because I'm dyslexic. I'd have a lot of anxiety going into school, especially for anything where we'd be reading out loud. And when I was eight years old my parents split up, so I was quite an anxious child, but the thing that really gave me so much joy was music. I would find the positives in everything and be upbeat and smiling, and much of that, I think, was because I had music as an escape and I was never afraid of having big dreams.

"The idea of music kept me smiling, and at night, when I went to bed, it kept me excited for the next day."

People would tell me that a career in music was way too big a dream, that we didn't know anyone in music, and that music wasn't the kind of thing that our family did. But that just pushed me more. The idea of music kept me smiling, and at night, when I went to bed, it kept me excited for the next day. Whether I was watching MTV or listening to the Official Charts, music was always escapism for me. And it meant that when I was a teenager, I pestered record labels for work experience. One of them, BMG (before they linked with Sony), called my mum to say that I had written them so many letters that they were going to have to let me come in, even though they didn't normally offer work experience. So from the age of about 15, every school holiday, I went in and did anything I possibly could – simple things like making the teas and coffees, photocopying, running notes around the offices. It grew this massive hunger in me and confirmed that music was where I wanted to be. I knew that I wanted to be on the performing side, but living the other side and seeing how record labels worked, how they signed artists and how they marketed artists, gave me a 360-degree view of the whole industry and I fell in love with it.

Q **Like you said, you were quite anxious. Are there any instances when you spoke up and used your voice, despite that?**

A A big part of that was in school. I went to the same school as my sisters, and it was reasonably academic. They pretty much expected everybody to go to university and to end up in a certain type of job. I had a meeting with my headmistress, who was such a lovely lady. She asked me

> **"But as I kept talking, I think she could see my passion and she realized it wasn't a joke."**

about what I was interested in for a career and for studying at university, and I remember a feeling inside my belly of, "Oh, I'm going to say the wrong thing here." I said I didn't necessarily think university was right for me and that what I wanted was to be in a pop band. Her face was a picture of complete confusion. She'd not had that answer before. But as I kept talking, I think she could see my passion and she realized it wasn't a joke. At school, no one ever laughed at me, but there was very much this attitude of, "Come on, be serious now. What are you actually going to do?" But I stuck to, "No, this is it."

I do think that to some degree you need that dedication and mindset to actually make your dreams happen, rather than relying on a plan B, because you need to give it everything you possibly can. I didn't go to a stage school, although I wanted to, and singing, dancing, and acting weren't things that my school was known for. So telling the headmistress that I wanted to do something so different felt quite scary at the time. But now, looking back, I think, "Well done." You do need to speak out for what you think is right for you.

Q **What a great lesson. Has anything else happened where you've had to listen to your gut like that?**

A After we decided we weren't going to put music out as the Saturdays any more, I was really lost for a few years. I missed seeing the girls – they were my whole world – and I missed performing. Then I went on *Strictly Come Dancing*, which was an amazing experience and helped to build my confidence back up. Then, off the back of *Strictly*, I was asked to come into Radio One and do a co-host with Matt Edmondson before shows. After the first three-hour show with Matt, I jumped in the car, called my mum, and said, "This has to be my career. This has to be it." Everything inside me was telling me that. But my career so far had been singing and performing, so I thought nobody would take me seriously as a presenter. And, as I'm quite anxious, that negative voice can sometimes become overwhelming. But even though the nerves and the anxiety can be very loud, I do think that your gut always knows what you want so I think you should trust it.

"But as much as you have the nerves, it's about picking yourself up, dusting yourself off and going again."

Q You're right. We tell ourselves to do things, but actually, how you feel when you're doing something – that's always a telltale sign.

A A hundred per cent. It can sometimes feel like a bit of a battle, can't it? Between your head and your heart, but what's going to make you feel excited to get out of bed in the morning? I've always tried to follow my heart, but it can be scary. It's not something you can do every day, but I like to think that if you listen to your gut as much as possible, then it will tend to lead you in the right direction.

Q You've touched on pushing yourself to get into a girl band and then changing careers. Do any instances come to mind when you've overcome fear? How did you do that?

A I'm a little ball of nerves most days. I try to talk to myself and say, "Come on. You've got this." On the first day at Radio One, I felt incredibly nervous. I'd been on as a guest before, and as an artist you know just what a big deal Radio One is. But to actually be on there, on the other side, as a presenter was really nerve-racking. And I felt pressure because I loved it so much and I wanted to prove that I could make the transition, though I knew it was something I'd have to grow into.

LISTEN TO YOUR GUT

It was also scary getting into the Saturdays in the first place. Like I said, I wasn't from a background where anyone was in music or performing. I'd had knockbacks in auditions before, and when you look around the hall and you see how many people are there auditioning, it's so nerve-racking. And I'm always my biggest critic. I'm always the first person to go, "Oh Molly, you hit a bit of a bum note there", or, "Oh, you could have sung that better."

But as much as you have nerves, it's about picking yourself up, dusting yourself off, and going again. I would be lying if I said that every time the mics go up at Radio One, I don't still get that butterfly feeling. If I didn't love this job and didn't care, I'm sure the butterflies wouldn't be there. But the fact is, I love it and I know how lucky I am. I don't want to mess up, I don't want to let the station down, I don't want to let the listeners down or make a fool of myself. So I'm always going to have a bit of the fear and have to try and overcome it each day.

"To an extent, I think you can practise being better at the way you think, and I wish somebody had told me earlier because I thought it was normal to be that stressed all the time."

KIA PEGG

"I've always tried to follow my heart, but it can be scary."

MOLLIE KING

"*I think maybe sometimes listening to your gut and doing the right thing pays off in the end.*"

AMY DOWDEN

INTERVIEW WITH

KIA PEGG

Kia Pegg is best known for her long running role as Jody Jackson in CBBC's *The Dumping Ground*. Kia can currently be seen as the latest recruit in The Mill Health Centre as receptionist Scarlett Kiernan in BBC drama *Doctors*. When Kia is not acting, she can be found as a regular guest presenter on CBBC and has also previously presented *Saturday Mash-Up!* Further credits include *Glue* (E4), *Horrid Henry* (Vertigo Films), and *The Legend of Dick and Dom* (CBBC).

Q How did you find your voice with acting?

A It's difficult to pinpoint the single point when I got into acting and presenting. I've been involved with performing since way back. My mum was a dance teacher and had been a dancer herself, so when she got me, she thought,

> *"As a kid, I was so sure of everything I believed in. I would never hesitate in telling anyone, but I struggled with that more as I got older."*

"Amazing, I can teach her to dance – this is going to be beautiful." She took me to her dance lessons, but I was really bad. I had no sense of rhythm, but also I'd get bored and be really chatty. I'd tell stories and act things out. So after that they sent me to a little drama group locally because I was really, really energetic and very full-on. I love to tell a story. I was really confident and super chatty. So I suppose that's where it began. Then my route into TV and acting for a job rather than just a hobby came through an amazing place called the Television Workshop. There used to be one in Birmingham, though there isn't any more. They took working class kids who wouldn't have otherwise had a way into the industry, and they trained them up. They used to go around schools and look for kids who had a bit of potential – which normally meant they couldn't behave themselves. When I was seven, they wrote to my school and my headteacher was like, "Have this one. She can't sit still. She can't shut up. She's an absolute nightmare."

Sadly, the Birmingham Workshop was due to shut down because of funding issues. But I got really lucky. On the night we were doing a big play, I was offered an audition for my first ever job so I was transferred to the Nottingham Workshop. My whole life has been being in the right place at the right time and stumbling into situations. It's hard for me to pick the moment when I got into acting because there have been so many little things. They've just added up nicely for it to work.

Q What did your family think?

My mum was that lovely balance where she wanted me to succeed and do well, but only because that was what I wanted. Everything I did as a kid was under my own steam. My mum was supportive but in no way pushy. If ever I didn't want to do something, I just didn't do it. She would never tell me to think of the opportunity. In fact, she used to actively try and talk me out of things if the auditions were really busy because it was all a lot of hassle.

"What matters is that you've got a good brain, and you've got a mouth to say the thoughts in it."

Tell me about *The Dumping Ground*.

The first series of *The Dumping Ground* came out in 2012 so I started on it the year before. It was my absolute dream job. When they offered it to me, that's when we found out that I had to move to Newcastle without my family. Back then, they never told you when you were auditioning that getting the job meant moving away, on your own. They used to save that until after they'd offered it to you. I'd never even had a sleepover at someone's house and now I had to move to Newcastle without my family. I was 11 and I thought, "Yeah, I can do that. Where's my suitcase?" My mum wasn't sure it was a good idea and she tried to convince me out of it, but I thought "No, I have to go. I have to. Really, this is what I want." So she said, "You can go, but you can come home at any time."

> *"That's quite a sad thing – to be 14 and be wondering in the back of your mind whether someone actually likes you."*

Q So, you're 11. You know you want to act, but how were you able, at such a young age, to believe in your voice when your mum was trying to talk you out of it?

A As a kid, I was so sure of everything I believed in. I would never hesitate in telling anyone, but I struggled with that more as I got older. My confidence left me for three or four years, between the ages of about 16 and 19. Although people who know me would probably disagree! But I know for a fact that I struggled at that age.

I grew up in a house where we were actively encouraged to speak our mind at all times. It wasn't expected – it was demanded – that you said what you thought. So I carried that with me into the world.

I'm very short – about five foot two inches – and I was the only girl in a home with two brothers. I think my mum looked at me and was worried that I looked like a fragile child, so she ingrained it into me that it doesn't matter that you're little. It doesn't matter that you're a girl. None of it matters. What matters is that you've got a good brain, and you've got a mouth to say the thoughts in it. I got pushed around a bit because I was very little, but I didn't care. I would just think, "I can do whatever I want." So I've been very lucky, really.

"My whole life has been being in the right place at the right time and stumbling into situations."

Q **What was school like? You were a child actor with this amazing voice, and you were being empowered by your mum at home, but you were doing something completely different to a lot of your friends. How was that?**

A I struggled with school a lot. It was odd to be an actor and go against the grain, but actually I think I would have struggled even without that. I had very unique interests: I'm a really big reader and am quite geeky, but super confident and very loud about it.

Just the other day, one of my best friends was saying how I never seemed to care at school that I didn't fit in. I think, in a way, it was because I wasn't even aware that I didn't fit in. I operated on my own and did my own thing. But I did struggle. I wasn't very popular, and I didn't have a very good group of friends. For quite a while I didn't really care about that, to be honest, but as I got older and wanted to make friends it meant that I found it difficult to gauge what was real and what wasn't. I could get along with people easily, but I knew I wasn't being true to myself, and we weren't really proper friends. I never quite knew if people wanted to be friends because of me or because I was on TV and had lots of followers on Instagram. And that's quite a sad thing – to be 14 and be wondering in the back of your mind whether someone actually likes you.

I think it's taken me a long time to realize what friends actually are. It wasn't until I was about 19 that I made a group of friends around whom I was fully comfortable to be myself. So it did take me quite a while. But once you've made that realization, you've got it for life. As long as you can get that and know it to be true, you're set.

Q If you could talk to six-year-old Kia, what would you tell her? Is there anything you wish you'd known younger?

A I've got a really overactive brain. It's like a carousel, rotating around and around, and coming up with different problems. Up until about a year and a half ago, I thought that was just the way my brain functioned and that I had to live with it. But then I questioned why I was allowing my brain to do that, and I actively started working against it and being more positive. To an extent, I think you can practise being better at the way you think, and I wish somebody had told me earlier because I thought it was normal to be that stressed all the time.

"I only valued myself based on the job I was doing at the time. And that's not the way to live."

I had to get into the habit of being happier so now I have a journal and I write a list of things that I'm grateful for each day. Sometimes they're big things like a really good day at work or landing a new job, and sometimes they're a trip to McDonald's and a really, really nice coke. This has been a huge turning point in my life. When you can be grateful for what you've already got, it's so much easier to be positive about what's to come. If you're miserable with what you already have, it's hard to find what's going to make you happy.

Q **What would you say are your biggest achievements?**

A For a long time, I struggled because I placed all my self-worth as a person on my work. So if work wasn't excelling, then I didn't allow myself to have happiness in any other area of my life. I only valued myself based on the job I was doing at the time. And that's not the way to live. If you have a bad day at work, you think it means you're an awful person and it's difficult to function. So now I actively put effort into splitting my achievements into those that are work and those that are me.

So at work, I've actually achieved some cool stuff. I was nominated for a BAFTA award when I was 14. That's the kind of big thing you're meant to answer: everyone strives and loves the idea of getting an award. But it doesn't actually change anything. It's not like when you're at work and somebody turns to you and says thank you for something you've done for them, or when the director of photography stops you on the way out to say, "By the way, I think that scene's really good." When someone I work with day-to-day says, "Can I just say, I really enjoyed your performance today", it feels more personal than collecting a trophy.

Currently for me, a really big achievement professionally is the presenting, and I'm educating myself about it. Again, I stumbled into it by chance after being asked to guest-present *Saturday Mash-Up!* I don't know why they asked me in the first place because I'd never done it. But it's amazing. I was brought up on CBBC so to turn up there and say, "Welcome to CBBC HQ" is such an adrenaline rush. I dance around like a toddler. And I'll be in debt to Harpz Kaur – the radio DJ and TV presenter – for the rest of my life. She got me through my first presenting job. I didn't have a clue what I was doing, but she gave me a crash course and got me through.

Outside work, I got a dog in the summer. My life revolves around this little black-and-white dog. He's called Kermit – I'm a huge fan of the Muppets. I've worked on training him so when I take him out in public and he behaves and is this lovely little dog to be around, it brings me so much pride.

"When you can be grateful for what you've already got, it's so much easier to be positive about what's to come."

There is one more thing I'm proud of. When I was a child growing up on *The Dumping Ground*, I had a good time. I loved it and I wouldn't trade it for the world. But I like to think that, when I was about 16, I did good things for the kids who were younger. Because I'd been in their place, they would often come to me for advice, to ask me to sort things out or to speak to the producers. They might say, "This has happened to me online. Do you know what I should do?" And I'd say, "Yeah, I'll put you in touch with the right people." When I was as young as them, I wouldn't have gone to an older cast member with any problems; I would've been ashamed to be struggling with anything. So I'm proud that I've matured and made myself someone who people trust and feel comfortable coming to with their problems. I must have done something right along the way for them to feel they can do that. It's nice to be in a position where you feel people want your help and trust you, and I'm proud of that.

AMY DOWDEN

Amy Dowden is one of the stars of the popular TV show *Strictly Come Dancing*. Amy started dancing at the age of eight, but it wasn't until after completing her A-levels she committed to it full-time. Alongside her partner (both in life and on the dance floor) Ben Jones, she achieved her dream of becoming British National Latin Dance Champion in 2017. In 2019, Amy announced that she has suffered from Crohn's disease since she was a child. She did this in conjunction with the launch of the It Takes Guts campaign run by Crohn's & Colitis UK, which promotes awareness of the disease and encourages sufferers to be open about their illness. Amy also runs the Art In Motion Dance Academy in the West Midlands with Ben.

Hi, I'm Amy. I'm from Caerphilly in South Wales, and I'm a twin. My twin sister, Rebecca, is my best friend, and I have a brother, Lloyd, who's three years older. As a young child, I was super energetic. My parents would say that I wouldn't even sit still for a cartoon. They got me into every little toddlers' club going to try and keep me busy, and obviously I'd be pulling Rebecca, my sidekick, along wherever I went.

In school, I was super conscientious. I wanted to be the first to finish my work, never wanted to be told off, and was super early for everything. I was a people pleaser, I guess. We were very family orientated – my cousins, my aunties, my uncles, and my grandparents were all just a walk away. My granddad had a static caravan in Cornwall so we were very lucky to go on lots of holidays down there.

My parents are very hard working. My dad's a carpenter. My mum works in accounts. And they dedicated their lives to us children. Lloyd, Rebecca, and I are extremely grateful, and we'll never be able to repay them for everything they did for us – for their belief in us, their focus, and their hard work.

"I loved it: I loved the attention, the spotlights, the music, the applause. I was in my element."

Discovering dancing

But anyway, going back to my granddad having a caravan – that's how I got into dancing. Every summer there was a disco-dancing competition. One year, it was my eighth birthday

> *"It was never easy, but I was so passionate."*

and I won – probably only because I had the biggest birthday badge on. But I loved it: I loved the attention, the spotlights, the music, the applause. I was in my element. I think my parents were a bit taken aback about where this Amy had come from.

After that, I begged my parents to take me dancing. They found a dancing school in Caerphilly and they'd take me and Rebecca – obviously my twin sister was going to come with me – on a Saturday morning. But little did they know it was about to take over their lives. I remember walking in and seeing all the little dance shoes the girls were wearing and meeting my teachers – who are still my teachers to this day.

And that was it then. I'd dance in the playground, I'd dance up and down the shops, and I'd wait all week for my Saturday dance class. The world of ballroom and Latin dancing can be very elitist and is a big financial commitment. I come from a very working-class family and my parents wanted to give us all the same. I could have been up and down the country doing lessons and competitions, but we couldn't afford that. The teachers knew, and I'm very grateful to them; they really took me under their wing.

Desperate to dance

When I was 11, I went to St Martins comprehensive school with all my friends – and Rebecca, obviously. But then, when I was 12, I was like, "No, I want to dance more." So I applied for scholarships for dance schools in London, but my Mum was like, "Amy you're not going to London." So then I found another secondary school in the area which had a dance department and was building a leisure centre with a dance studio. The school was full, but somehow I went there before term started and convinced the head teacher that I was going to be starting at that school the next day.

It was quite a big step to leave my twin because we'd done everything together. But it was also good because we became our own individuals with our own friends, but also we really appreciated the time we had together.

At the school, I got to dance more and I could do ballet and other forms of dance. The PE teachers would laugh because they'd just be sat down to eat their dinner and I'd knock on the door asking, "Can I go into the studio yet?"

Dedication and hard work

I was still very conscientious in school. It didn't come naturally to me, but I worked really hard so I came away with A stars, A's, and B's. Then I thought I was going to dance college, but my careers advisors and my parents all said, "No, get your A levels", because I needed something to fall back on. So I said, "Okay, another two years", and I was lucky enough to come away with straight A's at A level.

So there I was on A levels results day being interviewed for the newspaper, and they asked me what my plans were now. I'd applied for scholarships in London, but also for university because I had people pushing me to go down the academic route, but I told the paper that I had an interview later for a job as an office junior. Everyone was looking at me like, "What?!" "Yes," I said, "so I can fund my dancing. My Mum said she'd give me my wings, and I can fly now. I'm going to go dance." I know, secretly, my dad was like, "Come on, do it", because he knew how passionate I was, but some people though it was just stupid.

I found a boy partner from the West Midlands so I was able to compete, alongside doing my full-time job. I used to work in Cardiff five days a week until half past five. On a Tuesday and a Friday I'd then get in my car and drive two and a half hours to Birmingham to practise. He'd come down Wednesday. Then I drove to London on Saturdays, and we had competitions all over the UK on Sundays. I did that for three years. Even while I was studying A levels, I had jobs to fund my dancing. I worked in Pizza Hut, in a hair salon for £1.20 an hour, behind a bar, and I taught dance. It was never easy, but I was so passionate.

When your gut says "No – not now."

When I was 18, I had the option of going to London to dance on a scholarship, but I had the burden of an ongoing health condition. When you're in pain, the first people you want are your mum or your dad or twin sister, and being so far away from them scared me, I guess. And it was the right thing not to go because I was so poorly when I was 18 and 19, I wouldn't have got through the first year, or even the first term.

Health challenges

It was Christmas Eve, I was 11, and the bubbly energetic Amy who couldn't keep still was lifeless and kept passing out. For eight years I'd have these long episodes where I'd be very poorly for six weeks with my stomach, and then I'd be okay, but we didn't know why. When I was 18, it came with a vengeance, and a month didn't go by when I didn't spend at least a week in hospital. And then when I was 19, they transferred me to a London hospital. I spent six weeks there and I finally got diagnosed with Crohn's disease.

"If it wasn't for my condition, I'm not sure I would have achieved what I have. It gave me the strength and the determination to prove myself to everyone."

Crohn's disease diagnosis

Knowing what was wrong was a relief because I finally had answers, but I was probably a little bit deluded thinking that now we knew what it was I was going to be much better and I could finally reach my dreams. I didn't realize that no – this was just the start of a few tedious years for me learning about the condition, understanding my body, and accepting it.

There were times when I was 18 when I could see my dancing dreams fade away because I was in and out of hospital and wasn't progressing. But I guess I never lost hope. Knowing how it felt to have my dancing taken away made me more determined. Everyone used to say, "Oh she shouldn't be dancing with it." Even medical professionals. But I thought, "How dare they? They're not in my body. They're not living with it. How dare they tell me what I can and cannot do!"

I think there's a little bit of Amy that if you tell me I can't do something, I'll purposely try and prove you wrong. If it wasn't for my condition, I'm not sure I would have achieved what I have. It gave me the strength and the determination to prove myself to everyone.

"Listening to yourself, not others' opinions, pays off when you make decisions that you have to live with the rest of your life."

Big decision time

Another time I had to listen to my gut was when I had a big decision to make. Every dancer dreams of winning Blackpool – it's the biggest competition in the world. My dance partner and fiancé, Ben Jones, and I were working towards it. But *Strictly Come Dancing* was also a dream. I'd watched it on the telly since I was a young girl and had been inspired watching all the pros. And then the opportunity for both my dreams came at the same time, but I had to choose between them.

Ben and I were lined up to do the competition in the November and in the May *Strictly Come Dancing* contacted me. I was absolutely stunned. At the time Ben and I had several jobs, we were living in his parents' house, we were in debt, always just finding the next bit of money for our costumes and the next big competition. *Strictly* were amazing, they contacted the British Dance Council to see if I could do both, but the timings didn't work.

Ben and I had been together for several years and he'd worked his whole dancing career up to that point, and I couldn't have lived with myself if I'd taken his dream away from him. *Strictly* was an amazing opportunity, and so many people said to do it, even my parents. Honestly, turning down *Strictly* was the hardest decision I ever had to make, but I had to stay true to myself. I couldn't do it when I was taking that dream away from Ben.

Listening to my gut pays off

But still, there was no guarantee that Ben and I would go on to win the British Championships. In a competition, you never know what's going to happen. A new couple can come, couples can split and change up, the panels change, the new judges might not like you. Or it could just not be your night on the night. But we were lucky and we did win. *Strictly* emailed me saying they had all cheered in production when they found out.

After that, I didn't hear anything for months, but then I got the call, "Is this year a good year?" I couldn't believe it. I think maybe sometimes listening to your gut and doing the right thing pays off in the end because I was lucky enough then to get both the championship and *Strictly Come Dancing*. And I think looking out for others is looking out for yourself. Listening to yourself, not others' opinions, pays off when you make decisions that you have to live with the rest of your life.

Speaking up

Having Crohn's disease was something I never wanted to advertise in my late teens and early 20s because I didn't want it to define me. I didn't want people to say that I'd only been given an opportunity because of a health problem. And on *Strictly*, I wanted to be known as Amy the dancer, not Amy with Crohn's disease. I wanted to be recognized for the hard work I'd done and I guess I was scared that celebrities may not want to dance with me.

My close pros and production knew about it, but it wasn't something I went public with. Then I got a letter from a little girl whose mum knew me from a school I'd taught in. The little girl had just been diagnosed with Crohn's and she sent this letter that said, "You're amazing for achieving your dreams

> *"Speaking out about my condition was really tough for me, but it was probably the most rewarding thing I've done."*

of being on *Strictly Come Dancing* and having Crohn's disease... You've made me realize I can achieve my enormous dream of being a vet."

The letter made me want to speak out and raise awareness about Crohn's disease because there could be other little girls and boys or teenagers or adults who have a dream and are scared because they think the condition could stop them.

I helped on a campaign with Crohn's & Colitis UK called It Takes Guts, and now I'm a really proud ambassador. I do as much as I possibly can to break the stigma, to talk about it, to do what I can for young ones who've been diagnosed with it. Maybe some have had to miss terms of university or go back a year, but teaching them that my dream took longer but I got there in the end hopefully helps them not to give up. I went on to do my documentary, and I really made myself let people in and see me at my most vulnerable. Speaking out about my condition was really tough for me, but it was probably the most rewarding thing I've done.

"It's nice to be in a position where you feel people want your help and trust you, and I'm proud of that."

KIA PEGG

"Knowing how it felt to have my dancing taken away made me more determined."

AMY DOWDEN

LISTEN TO YOUR GUT

"Turning down Strictly was the hardest decision I ever had to make, but I had to stay true to myself."

AMY DOWDEN

OVERCOME FEAR

OVERCOME FEAR

It seems to get harder to overcome fear the older I get. Fear is a hard subject to tackle as it is not quantifiable and can sometimes feel irrational. Fear can be a good way to detect when something doesn't feel right for you. But learning how to decipher what is really fuelling your fear (it could be something truly harmful or simply something new and uncomfortable) is important. Trust me, there is a way to navigate that crippling feeling and not let it rule your life. Many people have felt the things you feel, and they too found a way to face that fear and forge on anyway.

ZARA MCDERMOTT

Zara McDermott is a presenter for the BBC, most recently having shared her personal experiences in two investigative documentaries for BBC3 entitled *Zara McDermott: Revenge Porn* and *Uncovering Rape Culture*. Zara's documentary explored the criminal acts of sharing or threatening to share private sexual images without consent. Zara is set to release her third project with the channel, a dating series called *Love In The Flesh*. Zara continues her campaigning work around revenge porn, and has joined the Duchess of Cornwall at an anniversary event for Refuge charity as well as a sexual assault referral centre as part of the NHS campaign.

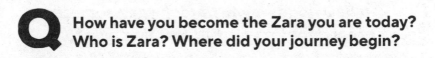

Q How have you become the Zara you are today? Who is Zara? Where did your journey begin?

A Zara as a child was quite shy, a bit of a tomboy. Never felt like she quite fitted in. I remember all the girls in primary school wearing these frilly skirts and pretty blouses, and I had no interest in any of that. I was the only girl in the whole year who wore trousers and refused to wear a skirt.

I never felt like I fitted, and I always struggled to find people who really got me – who were on my wavelength. And I suffered a lot of bullying in school, from Year 7 until I left in Year 13. I've moved on now from thinking that there's

> *"I've moved on now from thinking that there's something wrong with me – I think I was just very unlucky with the types of people that I came across."*

something wrong with me – I think I was just very unlucky with the types of people that I came across. The bullying meant that I wanted to get out of the education system so I went straight into work, and I spent three years in the Civil Service working for the government. That really changed my life in a lot of ways. I made so many amazing friends who are still my friends to this day, including my best friend in the whole world. During those years, from 18 to 21, I learned so much about how to behave, how to conduct myself, how to be an adult, and I learned that not everyone is going to be horrible. Not everyone has a vendetta against me.

When I was 21, I went on a reality TV show. I got a random message one day on social media about coming for a casting for a massive show. Initially, I said no. And then after

> *"If someone says "Jump", I say, "How high?" I'm still learning that that's not the right way to be."*

the casting, I said no to the show because I didn't think it was right for me. I've never been the loudest person in the room. I'm not the most outspoken person so I didn't think doing something like that would fit my personality. But in the end, after some convincing from my friends and family, I decided to do it. And it was incredible. I kept thinking about that 11-year-old girl, who had been just a shell of herself, stepping onto that TV screen for the first time and being confident. Though it wasn't actually real confidence – it was definitely a facade of confidence.

I had a lunch with one of my producers a few weeks ago, and he said that from when I got up in the morning on set on the first day of the show, I didn't say a single word until 12.04 pm. Wow. I didn't talk because I was so nervous. So shy Zara was still very much there at 21, and she still is today.

Q I love that because this book is for young people, and it's really important for them to understand that being shy and being bullied doesn't determine that you're not going to be successful later on in life. So thank you, I appreciate that. Is there any moment – as an adult or when you were younger – where you had to use your voice to speak up for yourself? Or maybe for your friends?

A That's a really hard question for me because, if I'm honest, I think I'm still learning to do that. I want to sit here and say, "Yes, there've been moments in my life where I've been firm and said, 'No, that's not right.'" But in reality, I'm still really learning to do that. I'm the biggest pushover in the world. If someone says "Jump", I say, "How high?" I'm still learning that that's not the right way to be.

So, I can't really think of an example. A good place to start, I guess, would be school, but I can't even explain to you how badly bullied I was, to the point where I was a shell of myself. I didn't have any capacity to stand up for myself

"Sometimes you can just say "no", and there's no need for excuses."

because I felt that I was always wrong. As I'm getting older, I'm much more confident in terms of the person I want to be. And I think the most powerful word in the world is "no". And my boyfriend always tells me this is the best word you can ever say to anyone, whether it's in TV, whether it's

> **"Sometimes you have to just throw yourself in the deep end, even if it seems like the scariest thing in the whole world. You've just got to do it because if you don't do it now, then when will you ever do it?"**

in your career or whether it's to friends or family who might ask for something that you can't give. Sometimes you can just say "no", and there's no need for excuses. Sometimes there's no need to give a reason. That's something I've learned, but I can't really think of a specific example when I've done it.

Q Thank you, that's so honest. There is no right answer. And I think that's a great response because we're all works in progress. If something feels wrong I'll try my best to navigate it, but it's not always easy. Are there any moments you can think of when you followed your intuition and you were proud of that?

A When I was making my first revenge porn documentary, there were so many times when it was really hard to be totally honest and vulnerable talking about something that has affected my life so much. In those situations, I really had to listen to my gut and reassure myself that it was the right thing to do and hopefully it would help people. Making that film was definitely a process of trusting the journey I was on and putting my trust in telling my story. I guess I felt my gut was telling me that this was the right thing to do. "You're doing the right thing. You're doing okay. You're gonna be fine." And actually, letting go of every teeny tiny doubt was the best thing I ever did – but it also took a lot of inner strength.

Q Did you have a moment when you were scared and thought, "Oh my gosh, I don't know if I can do this. Or if I should do this"? Are there any moments when you've overcome fear?

A Yes, there are so many moments when I've overcome fear. Every time I've done anything public facing – being in front of a camera, talking in public or being live on TV. And to be honest, I would go back and tell my younger self to start doing that by speaking up at school and offering to read in class. I never used to do that – I would sit back and be scared. And then, when I actually had to do that, in the real world, in my career, it was so scary. So I guess I've overcome a lot of fear. I think I've done it by not thinking too much about it. Sometimes the more you overthink it, the bigger chance it has of going wrong. It's better to just do the preparation, go to sleep, be well rested, get up in the morning, and just do that scary speech or that live TV moment. Don't overthink it, don't over prepare, and don't complicate it too much. Just let it happen. I would way

"You might be feeling a certain way right now, but, guaranteed, in six months' time, you'll look back and you'll be in a totally different place in your life."

rather someone turned up at my door and said I had a live TV appearance in 10 minutes than having a month's notice. Sometimes you have to just throw yourself in the deep end, even if it seems like the scariest thing in the whole world. You've just got to do it because if you don't do it now, then when will you ever do it? When I sang for the first time in front of millions of people on television, it was scary. I sang in front of Simon Cowell, other judges, and all of these amazing people. I saw JoJo in the audience – JoJo, the iconic musician I used to listen to when I was younger. That was the scariest thing I've ever done, but I know that I did it.

Q **What would you say to young Zara now? What advice or bits of inspiration would you give her?**

A I would tell my 11-year-old self not to be belittled. Not to let other people dishearten you over who you are. I would tell myself to never apologize or feel bad for being the person that you are, because that person is going to go on to make you the person you are in 10, 15, 20 years. It's okay to make mistakes, it's okay to learn things for the first time and figure out who you are. I spent so much time when I was younger wishing that I was someone else, wishing I looked like someone else, and wondering why I didn't get the attention that some people got and why I didn't have as many friends as other people. I constantly compared myself to others. There's so much life beyond being young, so much life to be lived. Nothing ever stays the same for long – that's something my mum always said to me. You might be feeling a certain way right now, but, guaranteed, in six months' time, you'll look back and you'll be in a totally different place in your life.

"Letting go of every teeny tiny doubt was the best thing I ever did – but it also took a lot of inner strength."

ZARA MCDERMOTT

"You fall over again, you get up again. It's fine."

EDITH BOWMAN

"There's nothing wrong with having a conversation with yourself to help you through an element of fear."

EDITH BOWMAN

"The problem with your gut is your fear, so if you eradicate that fear and see failure as something you can learn from, then it's worth it in the end."

ROMAN KEMP

ROMAN KEMP

Roman Kemp is one of the country's youngest and most promising broadcasters. Roman has hosted Capital FM's breakfast show for five years and has interviewed some of the biggest names in the entertainment industry. Roman made the final of *I'm A Celebrity Get Me Out Of Here* in 2019, and in 2020 he began hosting *Sunday Best* on ITV with his dad, Martin, which came back in 2021 as *Weekend Best*. As well as this, they have appeared in *Celebrity Gogglebox* for the last two seasons. Last year, Roman fronted his own BBC One documentary, *Roman Kemp: Our Silent Emergency*, a very raw film around male suicide and mental health.

Q **Tell us about young Roman and how you became the Roman you are today.**

A When I was younger, I was very, very energetic. I wanted to make people laugh and I was constantly putting on shows for my parents, from re-enacting scenes from *Ace Ventura* or pretending to be Frank Sinatra and dancing around the house. I was obsessed with impressions. When my mum

> **"We would ask questions and be encouraged to speak up when we didn't understand things."**

met my teachers at parents' evening, she'd tell me that my teachers were more boring than I'd made them!

I think that part of me did kind of go when I went through puberty. My serotonin levels were low and I became depressed at the age of 15. That silly side of me is still there somewhere, but I've been dealing with depression for a long time now. Therapy helps. Funnily enough, when I did, *I'm A Celebrity Get Me Out Of Here*, it was the first time I felt like I was back being that person. I guess because I wasn't surrounded by any outside pressures and things like that.

I'm really grateful to my parents for everything they've done for me. The biggest things they taught me are how to be kind to other people, how to be understanding, and how to make your own decisions and have your own confidence. They told me that everything I did as a kid was great, which gave me confidence and the ability to talk to people and start conversations. And now that's what I do for a living.

Q Are there any moments that you can remember when you had to speak up?

A Well, as I say, confidence was big in our family, and it started with my parents. They brought my sister and me up as their friends. It was never "the kids sit on this table", "the kids eat off this menu" or "the kids don't join in on those conversations." So much so that parents at my school would complain to my parents, saying that us kids shouldn't be having certain conversations at our age or that we shouldn't know about certain types of things. It was purely because we were inquisitive. We would ask questions and be encouraged to speak up when we didn't understand things.

However, being outspoken did have its downsides. One of the first football games my dad took me to see was Arsenal playing Bradford at the old stadium in Highbury. I must

"If there are things that are an issue, I think it's best to just talk it out. Once you do that, it's out there in the open and the universe can do the rest for you."

have only been about four years old, and I had this huge amount of confidence. The stands were near the pitch, and we were very close to the goalkeeper, who was time-wasting. There were 30,000 people in the stadium, about 10,000 in our stand, and in a quiet moment, I stood up on my chair and shouted, straight to the goalkeeper, "Get on with it, you cheating ***." I swore, to which the goalkeeper actually turned around. The whole of the crowd ended up cheering for me. My dad was a celebrity at the time and was very much trying to keep a low profile. He sank into his seat and pulled me down from mine. So that was my first moment of speaking out.

"In the end, I just had to jump in and hope for the best."

I've always been very outspoken, not in a bad way, but if I feel like it's the right thing to do. When it comes to my mental health, if there are things that are an issue I think it's best to just talk it out. Once you do that, it's out there in the open and the universe can do the rest for you.

"I was scared of opening myself up that much about my mental health struggles."

Q Absolutely. You've been through a lot. You've mentioned being a really chatty and bubbly character, and then having to deal with the opposite of that, with depression. So what would you say was a moment when you overcame fear?

A I've overcome a lot of fear. When they first asked me to do the Capital Breakfast radio show, I was so scared that I actually said no initially. For me it was a really scary and daunting thing. I grew up listening to that show. It was the show I listened to every day. Every day on the school run, my mum would have it on in the car, or it'd be on in the bus. It's like it was part of me. It felt like too much of a legacy – I couldn't see myself in the line of names that had done that show before. I think I didn't sleep for about two weeks. I held it in such prestige. Also, I had to overcome the fear that people were going to think I was just there because of my famous dad. In the end, I just had to jump in and hope for the best. I'd done every show on the radio, I'd done all

my flying hours and I was ready for it, but that doubt in your mind can kick in, even at the top.

Another moment of fear was releasing the documentary I made about mental health. That was a really scary one. I didn't even watch it until a while after because I was so worried. I was scared of opening myself up that much about my mental health struggles and also about doing justice to all the people in the documentary and their stories.

"Openness can lead to humility, and humility is the greatest kind of trait that I think anyone can have."

I think both of those examples show a fear of opening up, whether that was going on the airwaves and talking or sharing mental health experiences. I think guys particularly worry about that. But, at the same time, openness can lead to humility, and humility is the greatest kind of trait that I think anyone can have.

Q **Incredible, thank you for that. Is there anything you wanted to add about a specific moment where you remember listening to your gut and it paid off?**

A I do listen to my gut most of the time. Something, again, that my parents always said is that there's nothing better than opportunity. With an opportunity, there's never a wrong decision. If it presents itself, jump in and try it out because if you don't try, you'll never know. The problem with your gut is your fear, so if you eradicate that fear and see failure as something you can learn from, then it's worth it in the end.

I left school at 16 and went straight into a full-time job in music. I remember asking my parents, "What do I do?" And they said, "This is your decision. And we'll support you." That's such an amazing thing that I'll always do for my children – no matter what decision they make, if they go with their gut I'll just be there to support them. Whatever the outcome may be.

EDITH BOWMAN

Edith Bowman is an award-winning radio broadcaster, podcast host, and television presenter. Born and raised in Anstruther, Fife, Edith worked at her parent's hotel before studying for her degree and working in local radio as both a producer and presenter for two years. Her broadcasting career took off when she sent a speculative showreel to MTV. The channel immediately signed her to work on news roundup *Daily Edition*, which led to co-presenting MTV's *Hitlist UK*. From 2003 to 2014 Edith was one of Radio 1's lead presenters, co-hosting the Colin And Edith Show with Colin Murray, then her own solo weekday afternoon show, and on to the Weekend Breakfast Show. Edith's radio career continues, and spans both BBC and commercial stations.

Q So, tell us about knowing yourself, from young Edith to the Edith that we know today.

A It's really interesting when you think about knowing yourself because life in itself is a constant journey, where you change and you learn from your experiences and from your mistakes. You learn about the things you want to revisit – and also the things you don't want to revisit. So long as

you're willing to accept your mistakes and, where you've involved other people, make those apologies, it can be an incredible learning experience. You fall over again, you get up again. It's fine.

As a young girl in a tiny little fishing village in Scotland, I felt claustrophobic. I needed to get out. I had a wonderful collection of friends, some since nursery, and they're still my friends, but I felt like there weren't any opportunities there for me. I was tough work as a teenager. I'm a mum of two boys, and I've had that thing where people constantly say, "Oh, do you want to try for another one? To have a girl?" And I'm like, "Are you kidding? I don't want to have one of me!" I actually apologised to my mum and dad recently.

I was at the kitchen table with them and my 13-year-old son. I'm going through that experience of watching him, trying not to interfere but being there as a kind of a safety net. It's so interesting watching him develop, physically but also mentally. He's changing so quickly; this poor little thing, at times, has no idea what's going on or how to react, and stuff comes out his mouth. You can almost see in his face that he's not sure where that came from or that he doesn't mean it. So, at the dinner table, I said something to him, and he kind of barked at me and it was like, "Whoa!" My mum and dad were there, and it was like some kind of weird flashback. I was just like, "Guys this would be really good time for me to say that I'm really sorry for what I put you through from the ages of about 14 to 18." It was actually a really nice moment for my mum, my dad, and me. We can joke about it now, but my mum was a saint.

"So when I'd get told, "you've not got this" or "you can't do that", it spurs me on to do it and prove people wrong."

It's been so interesting being a parent and seeing my kids grow and go through certain things. It's reminded me of myself and of those moments where, as a young person, you face different things, like making choices about what you're going to study for the next however many years – that's terrifying.

Q Like you said, we've all given our parents problems. When you were younger, in this place that was too small for you, did you know you wanted to do radio or was there another avenue that you started first?

A No, I didn't know what I wanted to do, even when I left school, to be honest. I was always involved in music. I was in a band at school, and I was in the local amateur dramatics society, though I never got any parts. I played Sandy the dog in *Annie* – that's the extent of my theatrical achievements as a teenager. But I loved that environment.

My mum and her family ran a little hotel in Scotland so I grew up there, and from a young age, I was always around older people and I was older than my years, I guess. There was definitely a bit of an expectation within the family business that we would all stay and work there, but I knew I needed to get out. I didn't know how or what the opportunities were – any idea of being on TV would have felt so far away and out of reach.

I did all right at school. I wasn't particularly academic, but I really loved sport. I played hockey and football so I applied to train to be a PE teacher. The acceptance letter was the jolt I needed to realize that this wasn't what I wanted to do, which was kind of terrifying. I'd left it late, but I managed to get into my local college to do a diploma in communication studies. The course covered so many different things that I loved. There was video production and radio production – things I'd never had a chance to actually do or study.

There was also a bit of journalism, Scottish law – which I found weirdly interesting – and art and design. A wonderful concoction of things that fell under communicating – verbally, visually, audibly. So I did that for two years and then that got me onto the second year of the degree in Edinburgh. And that was my ticket out.

In Edinburgh, I managed to get work experience at a local radio station purely by constantly hounding them about it with letters and phone calls. The work experience confirmed that this was good. I liked it. For those two weeks, I was a human sponge, wanting to learn about everything: filing CDs, making tea, watching the sponsorship and promotions team, sitting in on shows, and chatting to John, who ran the library and did the music programming.

The two weeks were a really amazing insight into how a radio station ran. I could see the opportunities and knew that was the path I wanted to take. But I'd had to fight to get this work experience, and it's been a bit like that ever since and still. I've never been a person who's had something really handed to them. I've never been a person who's expected that. I think it's because I grew up in this environment around my mum and dad where, if you wanted something, you worked for it. So when I get told, "You've not got this" or "You can't do that", it spurs me on to do it and prove people wrong.

"I'd normally shy away from this sort of confrontation."

Q I love that. Were there any moments when you've thought, actually, you've got to speak up about something and use your voice, even though it wasn't easy?

A All the time, to be honest. Quite recently, there was a work situation where something didn't go in my favour. That was fair enough, but the way that it was done was not. I didn't feel it was an acceptable way to be treated. The way I was brought up is that you treat people as you want to be treated yourself – with respect, with appreciation, and with gratitude. I would hope that I'm exactly the same on camera as off camera.

But when this thing happened, I felt like I needed to stand up for myself and let the people know that they are accountable for how they treat people. I'd normally shy away from this sort of confrontation. I still suffer a lot from imposter syndrome, I think

"You need to stand up for yourself."

because I've had to fight and work hard for everything. So it wasn't easy, but what made it easier was that it was with a co-host, and we both felt exactly the same. So we compiled some emails together that we felt were necessary to let people know that we'd felt disappointed and really let down by them, and that their behaviour didn't complement what they stood for so it felt like they were being slight hypocrites.

> *"I decided to live with it for a couple of weeks to see how it felt, but within a couple of days I knew it wasn't what I wanted."*

Q It's so great you can do that. But it's hard.

A We were on the phone together going, "Okay, we're gonna send this... we'll do it together... three, two, one." Right up to the last minute we were questioning whether we should send it. But of course you should. This matters, and you need to stand up for yourself. We don't have any God-given right to a job, but we definitely deserve to be treated in a certain way. And we just didn't feel that that was right. So it was hard, but necessary, I think.

Q I think that's a really great example. Have there been moments where you've followed your intuition and done something, or not done something? When you've taken a leap of faith?

A I walked away from a really good, secure job. I'd been lucky enough to be asked to host the relaunch of the Virgin Radio *Breakfast Show.* The boss at the time took me for a cup of tea to ask me to do it. My first response was, "Who with?"

And he was like, "No, no, just you." And I was like, "Oh, okay. What do you want the show to be?" and he said, "I want it to be your show. I want you, with your producer, to come up with what you want the show to be." So I had this amazing opportunity for nearly two years where they gave me a blank canvas. It was amazing and a great success.

Then a new boss was brought in, who basically swept all the pieces off the chessboard, and it didn't feel right to me any longer. I decided to live with it for a couple of weeks to see how it felt, but within a couple of days I knew it wasn't what

"I walked, and it was terrifying leaving that security, but in hindsight, it was best thing I ever did."

I wanted. It was really well paid and was a secure contract, and I'd not long had my second child, but it wasn't what I wanted to be doing. I walked away. I was like, "Thanks so much, guys, but I'm out of here. Thank you so much for the experience, but this is not what I signed up for. This particular show, and the commitment asked of it, isn't worth it for me. So I'm going. Good luck." I walked, and it was terrifying leaving that security, but in hindsight, it was best thing I ever did. Change is good. My biggest piece of advice to people is not to be scared of change.

Q **Agreed. Absolutely sound advice, thank you. Whenever you've done anything scary, how would you say you overcame the fear?**

A I don't think the fear ever goes away, to be honest, and you get an accumulation of fears. There's the work side of things, where you have the fear that work is going to dry up and you won't get hired. That's a constant thing, particularly being a freelance broadcaster without long contracts – though there's a freedom that comes with that as well. Because I love what I do and the variety, I can also get nervous about doing it. I think that's a sign that I'm still doing the right thing. And when I don't feel nervous, maybe that's when I want to move on to something else.

Then there's also the fear about how present I am with my kids. I just had this thing where I was asked to do a radio show for a couple of weeks in the school holidays. So I've been having to weigh it up. Do I do it? Or do I not? My boys

> *"When I don't feel nervous, maybe that's when I want to move on to something else."*

were amazing and said of course I should do it. They said we could do this and that at weekends and they could come up to London with me. And my husband was great as well. He said that it had to be my decision, that they can't make the decision for me, but they can talk it through. I think that's the thing: communication is the best way to overcome fear. Talk to the people involved – whether that's your family or people you work with – make sure there's an open channel of communication. Or even have a conversation with yourself. I'm really interested in that side of things – there's nothing wrong with having a conversation with yourself to help you through an element of fear.

I've got two kids and I'm really cautious about not talking too much about them, but I know it's really helpful and important for people to have a balance and not just be totally work oriented. The thing about being a working mum is the guilt. A friend was saying I should absolutely do the two-week job because the boys would be fine and it was a really good opportunity and I'd be wonderful. I said it was the guilt thing and she said to get over it. But it's not that easy. It's like in cartoons, where there's a little devil on your shoulders: "You're working how much this week? You're a bad mum." But I am present for my kids, and I think it's really healthy for them, particularly for boys, to see me as a working mum. To see how important work is to me and how much it's part of me. Because I've realized that for me to be a happy, healthy mum and woman, I need to be doing what I love.

"So I'd say, enjoy the process, learn from every experience and do what makes you happy – it's your life and you only get the one chance."

DANNY WALTERS

"Change is good. My biggest piece of advice to people is not to be scared of change."

EDITH BOWMAN

"Communication is the best way to overcome fear."
EDITH BOWMAN

"I'd done every show on the radio, I'd done all my flying hours and I was ready for it, but that doubt in your mind can kick in, even at the top."
ROMAN KEMP

"I've realized that for me to be a happy, healthy mum and woman, I need to be doing what I love."
EDITH BOWMAN

DANNY WALTERS

Danny Walters is a London-born actor who most recently played "Keanu Taylor" in BBC's longest-running soap opera, *Eastenders*. Danny also featured in ITV's award-winning comedy sitcom *Benidorm*. Danny's other television credits include appearances in BBC's period drama series *Call the Midwife* and BBC3's drama *Our World War*. Danny is also a talented theatre actor, having starred in *The Greater Game* at The Southwark Playhouse and *Spring Awakening* at the Pavilion Theatre in Brighton.

Q So, I'm going to start with the first question: how did you get to know yourself?

A That's a really complex question to answer. There've been so many variables in my life that have led me to where I am today, so it's hard to pinpoint when exactly my life changed and I become this professional actor that I am today.

When I was younger, I was really interested in drama, music, dance, and storytelling. I really enjoyed doing those things, and just had fun being in the moment and not thinking about the bigger picture or any longer term goals. Then, when I was older, I had to work out what to do with my life. When I left secondary school to do A levels, I had to look at myself in the mirror and ask, "What can you give back to society? What are you good at? What do you enjoy, first of all? And how can you make a career out of it?"

For sixth form I did drama and music, but I always had this voice in my head – I guess my my dad's voice – saying "Make sure you have a backup plan." So I studied business as well to please my parents, but I was always hell-bent on drama and music. I'm not saying I didn't appreciate my dad's advice, but I don't like the idea of having to have a backup plan in this industry because I feel like every job nowadays – as we've learned during this pandemic – is very vulnerable. There's no real security in any industry.

I was really driven and focused and very passionate about acting, so after sixth form I went to a theatre school. I still enjoyed it, like when I was younger, but the fun had changed. I wanted to absorb everything, I wanted to find out about new practitioners and new styles of acting, and I wanted to improve and work on things like my vocal range and my accents.

> *"When you're older, I guess you put up barriers and become your own worst enemy and your biggest critic."*

When you're younger, you just have pure excitement and joy in exploring, whether that's football or ballet, playing the piano or riding bicycles, drawing or anything you have pleasure in – you just do it because it's fun. I miss that now. When you're older, I guess you put up barriers and become your own worst enemy and your biggest critic.

That's why I'm really intrigued about being part of this project with the BBC. It gives me a chance to go back to my roots, where it all began for me, and to find that passion I had and the sense of fun. I want to showcase and share that with younger generations so they can find their path for themselves.

"Sometimes it's very scary to voice your opinion because you think you're alone, but actually, there's loads of people who probably have the same ideas as you."

> "It's about being brave. It's about being confident in the decisions you make and standing by the person you really are."

Q Have there been any times when you had to speak up for yourself?

A One moment when I really spoke up for myself was when I changed agents, though I know this is a delicate subject because in the industry you don't really talk about business and agents. Near the beginning of my career, after all those years of trying to convince people that I could make a living from what I loved doing, I had some success in a TV show called *Benidorm* on ITV. That job gave me a sort of confidence – I wasn't cocky or arrogant; it was just pure confidence – that I had done that and I'd achieved that.

I had a meeting with my agent, and we had completely different visions. Maybe I was a bit headstrong, but I'm very ambitious. I'm a grafter. I like to work and I like to tell stories. I wanted to learn more and work with lots of different people, but my agent was on a completely different page. Because I had this recent confidence, I told myself, "No, believe in yourself here. Stick with your vision."

In this industry, we know there are lots of examples where amazing, talented people get changed and altered to become somebody that they're not. I've always said I'd rather leave the industry than be moulded and shaped. So, I said to my agent, "You know what, if we don't have the same outlook then unfortunately I'm going to have to leave this agency." And I did. It was extremely scary, but I got picked up by another agent. And months later, I was doing theatre and I was on *EastEnders* and I've been working on great projects.

Sometimes it's very scary to voice your opinion because you think you're alone, but actually, there's loads of people who probably have the same ideas as you, so you find your community. That's not just in our industry, it's in all walks of life. If you voice your opinion, there'll be other people who hear, and there'll be unity in that. I had to be brave in speaking up. And for anyone reading this book, it's about being brave. It's about being confident in the decisions you make and standing by the person you really are.

"I had to listen to those nerves but also listen to my gut to believe that I could do it."

I think it's quite important for people to understand that only you know what's right for you. People might be well-meaning, but listening to your gut and knowing who you are is important.

Q Have you had any moments when you've thought, "Yeah, I've listened to my gut, and it really paid off"?

A I remember, there was one time. I was in a play and when I was about to go on stage, I had this weird moment. I was waiting in the wings backstage, and my head and my body sort of just shut down. I felt like I couldn't go on, like I couldn't do the job. It was a weird, overwhelming sensation that I wasn't good enough to be on that stage and perform in front of this crowd who had paid money.

I lost my self-belief. I was nervous and shaking. But then, I suppose, I listened to my gut a little bit. I listened to something deep within me that said, "No, you are meant to do this. You're meant to go on stage." I was able to recognize that I was nervous, and as soon as I realized that I was vulnerable and I was human, I told myself, "Well, you know what, this is quite a universal feeling. You're not a robot. You're not a machine. You're not Robert De Niro – just yet." I had to listen to those nerves but also listen to my gut to believe that I could do it. As soon as I took that first step and walked onto the stage, I became the character, and that feeling was gone. So, if you do have any negativity, recognize it, accept it, and then just let it go. That's what I've learned.

Q That's great advice. It really is. Sometimes we stick with something when it's bothering us, but it's OK to stop and say, "I'm nervous. Can I have this moment? I'm human." What other words of encouragement would you give to a younger you?

A I think you can feel that school is everything that matters in the world, but it isn't – there's a wider world out there with so many opportunities and fantastic people from different walks of life, of different ethnicities, from different countries. The school environment can be very toxic – it can be amazing, of course – but if it's toxic you can lose yourself a little bit. So I'd say enjoy the process, learn from every experience, and do what makes you happy – it's your life and you only get the one chance. It's gonna be a bumpy ride, but be yourself.

"So if I can help motivate or educate young people to follow a different path, then you never know, I might end up working with that person in 10 years' time."

When my agent spoke to me about this BBC project, I thought how good it would be if I could inspire and encourage people and even change someone's life for the better. I got in fights when I was younger because I was bullied and I had to defend myself a bit. So if I can help motivate or educate young people to follow a different path, then you never know, I might end up working with that person in 10 years' time. They might employ me on one of their projects or in one of their screenplays or something. I always believe you should put good energy out there and help people. I've been helped by many, many people over the years, so hopefully this book will help others.

MORE STORIES FROM THE BBC

MORE STORIES
FROM THE BBC...

QENDRESA ZENA

NEWS DIRECTOR/SENIOR TECHNICAL OPERATOR, BBC LOOK NORTH

My name is Qendresa and this is a story about the journey that shaped me and my life and how I grew resilient and determined to work for BBC News.

Kur isha 13 vjeqe, erdha në Angli me familjen time, pasi që mbijetuam luftën në Kosovë. Në atë kohë nuk dija të flisja pothuajse as një fjalë anglisht, nuk kuptoja asgjë, vetem fytyrat i lexoja per te kuptuar boten rreth meje.

(TRANSLATION: When I was 13, I came to England with my parents after surviving the war in Kosova. At that time, I spoke no English and didn't understand anything, reading expressions on people's faces to understand the world.)

Confused? At 13, I turned up at an English school and I didn't understand a word of anything being said. I knew the word for "apple" and "yes" and "no", but certainly not enough to sit in a geography class and actually understand anything. So, one day when a teacher asked me a question in class, not only did I not understand a word of what she was asking me, but I didn't even know how to say "I don't understand." So I blurted it out in Kosovan and the whole class burst out laughing! I felt my cheeks burning up and tears of embarrassment were on the brink of spilling out, but I didn't cry. I was determined not to.

You see, before that I had lived through a war and I didn't think anything could ever hurt me again. But, let me take you back to how I ended up in England in the first place.

When I was 10, just before my 11th birthday, war broke out in Kosova and we had to leave. We were herded to the train station en masse; thousands of people being led through city streets by armed and masked paramilitaries. Then we spent the night on the train station floor, waiting to be packed onto a train in the morning. There were thousands of us. I had never even been on a train. I remember waking up in the night, staring at the pitch-black sky and wondering where my friends were. Did Zana and Arta get out in time?

The train was packed. We couldn't breathe, let alone move. My brother had a panic attack and my mum and dad tried to help him breathe, holding him up to a window that wouldn't open. Someone was shouting out for a drop of water. It was chaos. But we made it out.

So, after a stay in Macedonia and a trip back to Kosova, I make it to England. I can barely speak English, so I can't exactly make friends easily, but I make it through school with great GCSEs and start applying to college. And my school careers advisor almost laughed when I said I wanted to work in the media industry. They advised me to choose something else to study in college because the media industry was too competitive.

I didn't take any notice and applied for my course anyway. I got in and go on to study media production in college for two years. But once again, my tutor tells me I'll never work in the BBC – it's too competitive.

Now imagine this: every time I took the bus to college I would ride past the BBC building and look at it like it was a fortress. The building was a place where someone like me would never be able to even get in, let alone work – but still, I was determined. At this point, I'd built some resilience as well. I didn't let people put me off just because they thought things were going to be difficult. Because I had this dream.

When war was raging, I would hear my parents talking about what was on the news and that we needed to trust it because it's not propaganda – it's on the BBC, and they don't lie. I decided then that I wanted to work for the BBC, I wanted to be the voice that told people's stories, their truths. I wanted to be like the reporters who were telling our truth to the world.

If you're thinking "Why is she telling me her life story? I don't care!"... Well, I'm hoping you will, because I didn't realize it at the time, but it was my determination and resilience that got me my DREAM JOB.

I've cut a long story short, but after dreaming of working there, I got a day to look around at BBC in Leeds. That was 15 years ago and I never left! The moral of my story is this: determination and resilience pay off. Dream big, because as they say, "If you can dream it, you can become it". So put the work in and you will make it. Because if I can do it, everyone can.

RACHEL TEATE

PRESENTER, BBC RADIO TEES

Have you ever been scared of getting something wrong? Scared of not getting something right the first time? Sacred of feeling and looking stupid in front of other people?

I have. I've had so many moments where I've felt like a huge failure and I've wanted the world to just swallow me up. It took me nine attempts to pass my driving test. Yeah, I know – nine! That failure felt very public at college; everyone else was zooming around without "L" plates long before I was. I put on a brave face and kept on going, determined I would succeed and, on the tenth time, I passed.

I suppose this taste of turning failure into success set me up nicely for a career in performing arts! When I was 21, I'd had a series of auditions to host a brand new children's TV show. If I did it, I was going to be Daisy Doo – a character who drove a steam train and found out the answers to children's science questions. For a girl from Middlesbrough, who wanted to be on TV, this was a dream come true. I had made it. I signed a deal for the first series, which would start filming the following January. As January got closer, there wasn't any news, then an email arrived saying the show didn't test well with an audience and it wouldn't be getting made. I was absolutely devastated. Once again, I felt like I'd failed. Maybe the programme wasn't good enough because of me.

As an actor you have to deal with rejection all the time – when I auditioned for CBBC's *Wolfblood* I didn't get offered a role. Then one Thursday night I was cooking my tea and I got a call saying they needed me to play the role of Kara and could I start filming the following morning. YES!

Someone needed to be replaced on the show quickly, and I was the one to do it! So, I was 24 and pretending to be 14 – and acting way cooler than I ever was when I was at school! I worked on some amazing TV shows. I was murdered in *Father Brown,* filmed on *The Dumping Ground,* joined a new series called *Boy Meets Girl,* and became a social worker on *Hollyoaks*!

Life moved on and I became a mum to the most amazing little boy, but by the time I was 30, my life looked very, very different to how I had imagined it. I experienced failure on a whole new level when my little boy and I moved back in with my parents in Middlesbrough. I'd lost all my confidence and the thought of any further rejection made me feel sick. I'd rather have taken my driving test again than deal with any more failure, and that's saying something!

I'd gone from being on TV, playing different characters for a living, to not even knowing who I was any more. I needed time to heal away from the acting world, so I got a job as a receptionist at a car garage. One Saturday morning in September 2019, I went to work as usual and put the radio on. As the music played and the presenter talked, I went about my day, and then the garage went quiet and I heard an announcement asking if you had what it takes to be a radio presenter. And I thought YES – this could be my chance to be a success at something I wanted to do and to be creative again.

I was given a sticker with the number 60 on it, and I had 60 seconds to tell a story and then I had to wait and see if I got three yesses. I'd prepared a story that sounded really professional about a local playgroup I went to, but as I walked into the spotlight my mind went blank. All I could think was, "Don't mess this up, Rachel'. My mouth kept moving but I had no idea what words spilled out. It must have been good enough because I got through to the final! The result was going to be announced live on BBC Radio Tees, with the winner getting their own show on Christmas Eve. When the moment came, I heard "And the winner is..." I didn't hear my name. I was devastated – hot tears fell down my face. I felt like a failure all over again and I spent the day feeling rubbish and lower than ever.

In that moment, I had a choice – continue to feel like a failure and let that define me or stop, take a moment, and realize how far I'd come, then use it to motivate me further towards my dream. I knew I wanted to be a radio presenter; this was my passion and I wasn't going to let failure get the better of me.

That's exactly what I did, and I am so proud to say I am now a radio presenter on BBC Radio Tees and a producer on Creative Lives On Air. I'm also part of the BBC Upload team where I find stories to bring to our listeners, and I absolutely love it. I'm part of incredible podcasts like the *Happiness Half Hour* and the *Homegrown Heroes Podcast*, and I've hosted festivals for BBC iPlayer. I've interviewed some really interesting people like James Arthur and Cherry Valentine from *Ru Paul's Drag Race*, and I co-hosted Stockton Fireworks with over 30,000 people. I've been interviewed for the *Radio Times*, and I love any opportunity to talk about how amazing my hometown is.

Not winning a competition, not being picked first, feeling like a failure, used to be things I dreaded. I know I'll have those feelings again, but I know exactly how to deal with them because now I see that the way you deal with those failures can lead to your greatest success.

HOLLIE SMITH

JOURNALIST, BBC RADIO CYMRU NEWS

Take a second to imagine a 19-year-old girl, walking across her university campus in the city of Oxford in her purple pyjamas in the pouring rain. She was scared, she was nervous, and she was upset. Tears were in her eyes and her hair was sticking to her face as she walked towards Student Services to officially drop out of university. Well, in March 2016, that girl was me. I felt like a complete failure that day. But little did I know it would be the day that changed the course of my life forever. You may be asking how did I get to the point of despair at university? Well to answer that I would have to take you back to the very beginning.

I was born in a town called Newport in South Wales in the late 1990s. Life wasn't always easy growing up. My parents shouted and argued constantly – they would have screaming matches until late into the night. Thankfully, my parents divorced when I was around seven or eight, but after the divorce, I had to move around – a lot (about 12 times before I was 16). Moving around so much made it hard to make friends, and I began to feel like I didn't belong anywhere. But I did belong in a world of stories. I loved to read and write, and would tell stories to my family and those around me.

I started out writing little newsletters for my mum, and as I grew older I knew I wanted to write and tell stories for a living. I wanted to be a reporter, just like my heroes on the news – journalists around the world, reporting from war zones and crime scenes. But to be a journalist, I knew I had to work hard at school and go to university. Back then, I thought the only way to become a reporter was to go to university and get a degree in something. I would've been the first person in my family to go to university. I was often reminded of this by my family and teachers. The pressure was on and I felt it.

My mum grew up in a large family with not a lot of money, and I grew up in a similar way – especially being the eldest of my siblings. Although we had the things we needed most of the time, things were tight. In going to university I would be making something of myself, and hopefully wouldn't have to worry about where we were moving to next or if we could afford certain things.

I loved to learn, and when I eventually got into university to study politics I did pretty well academically, too. But the university lifestyle came as a shock to the system. I felt alone, and couldn't fit in with people around me – especially as they came from wealthier backgrounds and had more experiences outside their own little hometowns.

Halfway through my first year, I felt sad and lost. I was lonely, and couldn't see my future any more – the future I had worked so hard for. I wanted to belong, but at the same time I wanted to run away. I remember a phone call I had with my mum before making the decision to drop out, where she reminded me that it wasn't worth seeing university through if I couldn't see myself any more.

And so, back on that rainy March morning, I tearfully walked over to the student services building to drop out of university, not knowing what the future would hold. I'd like to say that life immediately got better after dropping out of university – that it was my happily ever after. But I was soon back home, working a part-time job I didn't like, and I felt like a complete failure. I was still miserable.

A few months down the line, I realized I needed a change. And so I went on an adventure. I accepted a job overseas as an au pair in the United States. I travelled all over America making new friends, having new experiences, and facing new challenges.

During my time in the US I had some time off, and so I decided to take myself to a place I had always wanted to go: New York City. It was like a dream, for anyone who is wondering. It was just like it is in the movies, with the big yellow taxis and bright lights of Broadway. I remember finding myself standing outside the offices of the *New York Times* newspaper. I took a moment, and thought about all of the journalists who had worked there over the years. In that moment it felt like a flame had been ignited inside of me. I suddenly remembered that I wanted to be just like those journalists. I remembered my dream.

A few months later I returned to the UK after my time in America with a renewed sense of purpose. I applied to every job in journalism going, and was told "no" or rejected a lot in that time. But eventually I saw the BBC was offering a journalism apprenticeship, and I applied. After many months of waiting, I landed a place on the scheme. I was going to be able to work and train to be a journalist without ever having to go back to university.

Looking back on my life, there have been some really high highs, but also some really low lows – and those twists and turns often remind me of a river, and how it ebbs and flows. Sometimes a river level will be really high, but at times, it can be really low. But it's important to remember that the lows won't last forever. And just as the river continues to flow on, so will we.

JAX SINCLAIR

JOURNALISM RESEARCHER, BBC SCOTLAND

When I was seven I remember walking past a mirror. I thought at first it was one of those ones from a circus – you know, the ones that make you look all wavy – but it wasn't. I just couldn't recognize the face staring back at me. In fact I didn't recognize my face until I was 17 and staring into a mirror in my room in a supported living homeless shelter.

A lot happened in those 10 years, let me tell you. When I was in high school, we had to wear uniforms, much like the ones that kids wear now. The girls wore skirts and the boys wore trousers. I felt like a fraud in a skirt, so I wore trousers, but it didn't stop there. I didn't fit in with boys or girls. I thought perhaps I was actually an alien from outer space. People would call down the corridors, "Are you a boy or a girl?"

I was asking myself the exact same thing. It was as if my head had been imprinted with the wrong roadmap for my body at birth. A genetic malfunction.

I waited patiently in long grey corridors to be seen by CAMHS and then the Gender Clinic. They did tests and I had to speak to different doctors. Eventually they told me I had a medical condition called gender dysphoria.

Tracing steps backwards to my home, you would find old family pictures of someone I wish I didn't know. I was presented with a conversation I didn't feel hungry for. I tried to find the words that would make me clear, but nothing would come, only fear. I would have my phone taken away from me if I went to a barbers. They threw out my boxers and replaced them with knickers.

"Grow your hair out long."

"Wear that flower perfume."

"Slip into that dress." A straightjacket.

Within society's parameters, "dream big" – but dream only of what others dream for you.

I am human no matter what they shout, no matter how much they doubt or deny. It became an unhealthy environment for me at home, and I went into care. I stayed motivated and tried to turn the negatives in front of me into positives. I didn't want to be seen as just another statistic on a page.

I would make videos in my room to talk about my own transition. It was as if I was reaching out online to send a signal to see if anyone else out there felt the same as me. That signal reached the eyes of Scotland's health correspondent. She asked me if I would like to be interviewed for a piece on the Gender Recognition Act reforms debate. I agreed, but only if I was allowed to shadow her for the day. I am forever grateful that she continues to support me even today as my editor.

I managed to gain the qualifications needed to get into university while I was homeless. It was challenging; at times I didn't have the same access to Wi-Fi, food, or support that my peers did. However, I viewed education as being the key to unlocking a better tomorrow, so I ventured to study abroad in South Korea in 2020. When the UK government was calling us to come back due to Covid-19, I decided to stay. While I was there I filmed, presented, and edited a video for *Reporting Scotland,* telling the audience back home what life was like in Seoul during the pandemic. This gave me a hunger for storytelling. I graduated in July 2021. I woke up one morning to a ding – a ding I had been waiting on for weeks. When I opened my eyes, it was with disbelief that I viewed my final results. I had achieved a First-Class Honours degree in Journalism..

I now work at the BBC helping to make documentaries. The *Disclosure* team is teaching me how to uncover information that some people do not want you to find out.

I presented my first film in March. It is available on iPlayer and is called *Should I Tell You I'm Trans?* It's important for me to be visible; there aren't any open transmasculine broadcast journalists in Scotland. I want to be the person that I needed to see when I was growing up.

My journey has made me resilient. Over time, things became better with my family, too. I grew into myself and started testosterone and I was happier and able to maintain healthier relationships with the people around me. Rather than letting my experience of growing up trans prevent me from achieving my dreams. I made this work for me.

My story helps me to come up with ideas and connect with other people. I am looking forward to a future helping other people tell their stories, too. Don't let your story inhibit you – your story is your power.

Project Editor: Pamela Afram
Senior Designer: Clive Savage
Designer: Anita Mangan
Production Editor: Siu Yin Chan
Senior Production Controller: Mary Slater
Managing Editor: Emma Grange
Managing Art Editor: Vicky Short
Publishing Director: Mark Searle

Dorling Kindersley would like to thank James Stirling and Daniel Mirzoeff at the BBC,
Elly Dowsett for her editorial work and Lizzie Huxley-Jones for their authenticity review.

BBC ACKNOWLEDGEMENTS
With thanks to Fraser Fletcher, Patsy Goodwin, Hollie Smith, Proinsias O'Coinn, Yvette Twagiramariya, Bara'atu Ibrahim,
Chanise Evans, Emily Unia, Miriam Barker, Anisha Johal, Jenn Lenning, Adam Clarkson, Megan O'Neill, Emma Louise
Oldfield, Jack Lyons, Charlie Raine, Amelia Benjamin, Kamilah McInnes, Alva King, Luqman Tofey, Ben Woolvin,
Lucy Bolt, Kesewaa Browne, Carla Greene, Carmella Osbourne, Steph Watkins, Sian Davies, Rob Dowell, Rachel Teate,
David North, Mike Minnay, Jax Sinclair, Amy Macmillan, Anoushka Williams, Ellie Colton, Lizzie Hylan, Bek Homer,
Qendresa Zena, Carla Fowler, Gem O'Reilly, James Barclay Devine, Brigid Harrison-Draper, Lucy Baxter, Liam Richards,
Kim Boak, Ben Maeder, Amy Nomvula, Rosanna Skwarka, Angelle Joseph, Jacob Ottaway, Stacey Harcourt,
Gaz Drinkwater, Ian Marshall, Ross Fiddes, James Stirling, Amber Lily Mockridge, Lucy Wilson,
Rhona De La Mare, Natasha Prowse, Emily Kasriel, Emma Glendering.

PICTURE CREDIT
Picture of Nadia Jae on the cover and on page 10 courtesy of the BBC.

First published in Great Britain in 2022 by Dorling Kindersley Limited
One Embassy Gardens, 8 Viaduct Gardens, London SW11 7BW

A Penguin Random House Company
Page design copyright © 2022 Dorling Kindersley Limited.

10 9 8 7 6 5 4 3 2 1
001–331498–July/2022

This book is substantially a work of nonfiction based on the experiences and recollections of the contributors.

Jacket design by Anita Mangan

A CIP catalogue record for this book is available from the British Library.

ISBN 978-0-2415-6753-1

Printed and bound in Great Britain

For the curious

www.dk.com

MIX
Paper | Supporting
responsible forestry
FSC™ C018179

This paper is made from
Forest Stewardship
Council™ certified
paper – one small step in
DK's commitment to a
sustainable future.